super natural every day

HEIDI SWANSON

super natural every day

Well-Loved Recipes *from* My Natural Foods Kitchen

TEN SPEED PRESS
Berkeley

Published in the United States by Ten Speed Press,

an imprint of the Crown Publishing Group, a division of Random House, Inc., New York.

www.crownpublishing.com

www.tenspeed.com

Ten Speed Press and the Ten Speed Press colophon are registered trademarks of
Random House, Inc.

Library of Congress Cataloging-in-Publication Data

Swanson, Heidi, 1973–
    Super natural every day : well-loved recipes from my natural foods kitchen /
    Heidi Swanson.
        p. cm.
    Includes index.
    Summary: "A collection of 100 vegetarian recipes for nutritious, weekday-friendly
    dishes from the blogger behind 101 Cookbooks"—Provided by publisher.
    ISBN 978-1-58008-277-8 (pbk.)
    1. Cooking (Natural foods) 2. Cookbooks. I. Title.
    TX741.S8874 2011
    641.5'636—dc22

                              2010043749

ISBN 978-1-58008-277-8

Printed in China

Design by Toni Tajma

10 9 8 7 6 5 4 3 2 1

First Edition

CONTENTS

INTRODUCTION

I LIVE IN A MODEST SIX-ROOM FLAT with twelve-foot ceilings on the
second floor of a Victorian apartment in the middle of San Francisco.
And by "middle" I mean that if you threw a dart at the center of a map
of this city, you'd likely hit my house. My street dead-ends into an east-
sloping neighborhood park, and when you stand at the front window
you can watch a parade of pugs and pinschers, big kids on dirt bikes and
small kids on scooters, dealers, joggers, and the occasional flute player
go by. There are times when two girls set up a music stand in the shade
and practice trombone.

San Francisco is a vibrant city that punctuates the top of a fist-
shaped peninsula, contained on one side by the Pacific Ocean and
flanked by its namesake bay on the other two. It is where the North
American continent jets out of the sea in dramatic fashion before rum-
bling east. I've lived within a short drive of this coastline nearly all my
life, and at the right moment, on the right day, in the right spot, there is
no more inspiring place to explore.

Within reasonable walking distance of my front door, you'll find
plenty to eat and drink—paneer-stuffed *kati* rolls, freshly baked walnut
levain, Neapolitan-inspired thin-crust pizzas, and egg sandwiches served
on English muffins fresh from the oven. There is a teashop pouring
silver needle, *gyokuro*, and monkey-picked oolong teas nearby. And as
far as coffee goes, I often walk to one of the two coffee shops roasting
beans on their premises. There is a boisterous bar worth braving just up
the block with dozens of Belgian ales, IPAs, stouts, and hefeweizens on
tap. And when I'm in the mood for something more low-key, the beer
shop in the other direction has a similarly impressive selection in bottles
I can take home.

There must be two dozen places to buy groceries. Some are chains;
many are independently owned and small in scale. On any given afternoon I might stumble upon a box of purple rice grown by a workers'
co-op in Thailand on a shelf just a few feet from a jewel-toned jar of
locally produced bergamot marmalade. Or, farm-fresh eggs a few hours
old across the aisle from hand-harvested Mendocino nori. The farmers'

markets? There's one nearly every day of the week, and choosing which to go to depends on how far I feel like walking.

But as exciting as urban living is, I often feel the pull of quieter realms. Drive an hour from where I am right now, and you might find yourself in the midst of a redwood grove, or standing on a bluff overlooking the Pacific Ocean, or making snowballs at the summit of one of the neighboring peaks. There have been mornings in late spring when I've found myself traveling through wildflower-lined highways in west Marin County, poppies spilling from the ditches to flood the black asphalt. Farther inland, in the summertime, you'll find endless stretches of golden hills punctuated by the craggy silhouettes of old oak trees. In these moments, there are few places I'd rather call home.

I live here with my boyfriend, Wayne, and it's against this backdrop that I cook each day. The markets, shops, and restaurants define the palette of ingredients I reach for; they influence the flavors I crave. The hills and vistas, blooming flowers, and candy-colored houses—they shape my overall aesthetic sensibility and inspire me to highlight the natural essence of each of the ingredients I choose to use.

Super Natural Every Day

This book is a glimpse into my everyday cooking, with the hope that some of what inspires me will inspire you as well.

I resisted the urge to include over-the-top, special-occasion productions. I left out recipes requiring all day Saturday and on into Sunday to prepare, and skipped the ones with six different components. Instead, I kept a simple notebook over the past couple years of my favorite everyday preparations—ones I revisit often. The recipes are rooted in whole and natural foods, typically feature a handful of seasonal ingredients, offer some inkling of nutritional balance, and (broadly speaking) come together with minimal effort.

For those of you with *Super Natural Cooking,* consider this a companion volume. Many of the building blocks I outlined in that book are put into practice here. Simply put—here are real foods and good ingredients made into dishes that are nourishing and worth eating and sharing.

Natural Foods

If you peek inside my kitchen cupboards you'll probably notice I prefer my rice brown, red, purple, or black; and that I keep a spectrum of golden honeys close at hand. You'll see soba noodles are allocated a good amount of real estate in the cabinets to the right of the stove, and heirloom beans have taken over 2 feet of shelf space on the left. You might (rightly) suspect my favorite section at the grocery store are the bins containing grains, dried beans, and flour.

I tend to cook with whole, natural foods—whole grains, whole grain flours, minimally processed sweeteners, and fresh produce—ingredients that are as seasonal and nutritionally intact as possible. I'd be misleading you if I said I don't look forward to moments when I happen upon something new and special: a raw, vanilla-scented Fair Trade Certified cane sugar from the Philippines, or giant, golden salt grains from the Menai Strait in Wales. Those sorts of ingredients aside, a good portion of the food I buy is grown or produced locally. I find local ingredients taste better and often have a glow and vitality you don't see in ingredients that have traveled long distances, particularly when you are talking about produce or perishables. And while I run the risk of sounding a bit preachy, supporting good ingredients grown or produced by people who care about our health and the health of our environment is something about which I feel strongly.

Some of you might be confused by the term "natural foods." It is used in many different contexts, and it means different things to different people. By "natural foods," I mean ingredients that are straight from the plant or animal. Or that are made with as little processing and as few added flavorings, stabilizers, and preservatives as possible, keeping nutrients and original flavors intact. For example, wheat berries ground into flour, grated coconut pressed into coconut milk, cream paddled into butter, or chopped tomatoes simmered into tomato sauce. For me, focusing on natural ingredients also means doing my best to avoid genetically modified and chemically fertilized crops, as well as dairy products that come from cows treated with growth hormones. I want each meal I eat to deliver as much nutritional punch as possible, and focusing on a range of real, minimally processed foods is the way I go about it.

I occasionally use unbleached all-purpose flour or white sugar, usually in baked goods, when using 100 percent whole grain flours (or less refined sugars) doesn't quite deliver the results I want. For those of you who bake strictly with whole grain flours, I try to make note of what you can expect from using 100 percent whole grain flours in those recipes.

This is as good a place as any to mention that I'm vegetarian, and have been for a long time now. I'm happy to do what I can to leave a lighter environmental footprint on our planet, and I have enjoyed the challenge of shifting my way of cooking and eating to be lower on the food chain. For me, this means being vegetarian, buying a good percentage of my ingredients from local producers, and seeking out sustainably produced ingredients. That being said, it's each individual's own personal journey to work toward a way of eating that works for them. Many people seem to be looking for ways to incorporate more meatless meals into their repertoire for a whole host of reasons, and I'm happy to try to provide a bit of inspiration. Many of the recipes in this book, particularly the main dishes, welcome substitutions, and I encourage you to use some of the ideas as starting points. Go from there based on what is available in your area, or what your family likes to eat.

I think it's also worth mentioning that while I try to shop, cook, and eat mindfully, I also do my best to remember why I was drawn into the kitchen in the first place—the punch of garlic hitting me in the face after being dropped into a hot pan, the perfume of chocolate wafting from room to room when a cake is in the oven, the explosion of color I discover every time I slice into a blood orange, or the pleasure of sharing a simple meal I've prepared with a group of friends or family. These are the sorts of things that get me excited to cook each day, and I do my best to let them inspire my time in the kitchen before all else.

Where I Shop

The cornerstone of my food shopping is a weekly trip to one of the nearby farmers' markets. I stock up on whatever looks good, and typically this means a range of in-season fruits and vegetables, a dozen farm-fresh eggs (sometimes two), a container of locally made tofu, one of almond butter, and sometimes bread, if I haven't baked a loaf myself.

I shop alongside many of the best chefs in the city. They push their carts from stall to stall, and I love to sneak glances at what they are buying for their kitchens. There are times, if I don't feel like I'm imposing too much and if they don't look like they're in too much of a hurry, when I'll ask what they are going to make with those flats of asparagus or those bundles of sorrel. Often, the farmers are also a good source of information and inspiration. One of my favorite recipes in this book, Kale Salad (page 80), came out of a quick chat over a banged-up box of purple peacock kale. Another time, while gathering ingredients for posole, I received an impromptu lesson in how to choose the most flavorful tomatillos—pick the small ones, those that are firm, with a deep blush of purple inside the papery husks.

When running low on ingredients between market visits, I head to one of the little grocery stores near my house. One in particular sources produce from local farmers and has even started to grow a few crops outside the city.

Aside from that, once or twice a month I go to the local natural foods co-op or Whole Foods Market to replenish pantry staples: primarily interesting grains, flours, beans, lentils, and various rices from the bin section.

Then there are a sprinkling of less-frequent visits to specialty stores where I cherry-pick wines, or cheeses, or artisanal sugars, special spice blends, offbeat oils, and vinegars.

My Everyday Pantry

While my everyday cooking is most often dictated by seasonal produce, I need to keep a supporting cast of ingredients on hand so I can put that produce to work in a variety of ways. I went into a lot of detail about the minutiae of individual ingredients (and some of their nutritional benefits) in *Super Natural Cooking*—specifically, how to build a natural foods pantry. Instead of repeating that here, I thought I'd open my cupboards, look to my shelves and fridge, and tell you about what you are likely to find in my kitchen on a day like today.

Before we get started, just a few notes. I'm not going to call out "organic" in every instance throughout this book. I suspect that would get tedious and turn off some of you. What I will say is that I care about supporting producers and farmers who are using sustainable farming methods. Many of those are certified organic; some of them aren't certified, but are farming using organic practices. I read a report that over 160 million pounds of pesticides were sprayed in California in 2008, a statistic I find heartbreaking. I know we can do better, and I try to vote for that change with my grocery dollars. I buy dairy products from farmers who pasture-graze their growth hormone–free cows and I purchase eggs from farmers who keep small flocks of pastured hens. This is in part because I want to support the people providing these ingredients, and in part because I don't want to be in a supermarket at some point without a choice in the matter.

OILS AND FATS I cook with a variety of oils and fats, and pick and choose which to use after considering a few things. Each fat and oil has its own flavor, scent, and mouthfeel—I think about how each of those elements might affect what I'm cooking. I look for cooking oils and fats made from good ingredients, which have been naturally pressed or produced without stripping them of their personality. Avoiding oils that have been processed with solvents, deodorizers, or heated to damaging temperatures is important. Then, once in my kitchen, I think about how each cooking oil stands up to heat differently, and take that into consideration, too.

I keep a few **extra-virgin olive oils** on hand. Of those, I typically have one that could be considered my day-to-day olive oil. I use this to sauté, roast, make sauces, and form the base of a variety of dressings and vinaigrettes. The other extra-virgin olive oils are more special (and costly), and I think about them as finishing oils. Some are spicy, some are grassy, but they're all better enjoyed drizzled over soups, stews, or salads just before serving.

I like to cook and bake with butter, sometimes clarified, sometimes browned. You can make clarified butter yourself (see page 224) or buy it. Making it yourself is more economical. It has full, rich flavor and a substantially higher smoke point than olive oil. Certain curries really come to life when you use it to start things off, and you can combine it in a pan alongside olive oil to give the olive oil more range. I like to use **brown butter** (see page 225) in baking or for drizzling, as well as plain butter, both salted and unsalted.

Extra-virgin coconut oil is fun to experiment with, although its assertive coconut scent limits what I use it for. It's great for baking, and you can sometimes replace all, or a portion, of the butter in a recipe with coconut oil. I use it in the early stages of some Thai-style curries, and in just about any cooking that has coconut milk in it.

I use little whispers of **toasted sesame oil** in my cooking, but it can be devastatingly overpowering. To say I'm judicious with it is an understatement.

Cold-pressed nut oils are nice to have on hand, particularly in the fall and winter when the weather cools and heartier meals are in order. I look for cold-pressed, artisan pistachio oils, toasted pumpkin seed oils, hazelnut oils, as well as walnut oils. They should smell like an intense version of the nut or seed from which they were pressed. I don't cook with the nut oils per se, but use them in various nut-based purees, dressings, and *picadas*. Gentle heat helps to release their scent, and they shine drizzled over dishes like warm farro salads and just-out-of-the oven casseroles. Buy nut oils in small containers when you can, and store them in the refrigerator if they aren't in high rotation in the kitchen. They tend to go rancid in a flash and are expensive to replace.

QUICK-COOKING GRAINS **Quinoa, bulgur wheat, millet,** and **rolled oats** are popular around here. There are other quick-cooking grains, but these are the ones I use most often. Whole-wheat couscous, a tiny grain-shaped pasta, is great for quick salads and for stuffing vegetables like tomatoes or zucchini. You can find many of these, in organic versions, in the bin section of natural foods stores, and they tend to be very inexpensive.

LONGER-COOKING GRAINS I keep a range of **whole grain rices** on hand, as well as **farro, barley, wheat berries,** and **rye berries.** I think many people miss out on cooking with the larger grains because of the perception that they take forever to cook. This is only partly true. If you plan ahead a bit, it's nearly effortless. So, for example, I'll cook up a pot of farro on a Sunday afternoon, use it in that night's dinner, reserve some for use throughout the week, and freeze the rest. If you were to glance in my freezer, you'd find bags of frozen brown rice, farro, and wheat berries. I might use the wheat berries in a soup tonight, the brown rice in a stir-fry tomorrow, and the farro in a tart filling sometime later in the week. Again, most of these are available, in organic versions, in the bin section for just a couple dollars a pound. Farro tends to be pricier, but well worth it.

FLOURS I counted twenty-two different flours at the natural food store the other day—a number that is both exciting and overwhelming. I use a small subset of those flours in my day-to-day cooking. I use a lot of **whole wheat pastry flour** and **spelt flour** for baking. Both are capable of creating beautiful, tender baked goods. I do keep a bit of unbleached all-purpose flour around because, as I've mentioned before, there are times, particularly in certain baked goods, when I've found that using a percentage of all-purpose flour makes for a much better end result. If I need a bit more structure and less tenderness from a dough, I use **white whole wheat flour**, which is higher in gluten-forming protein—good for pizza dough and certain breads. Beyond that, I rotate through a number of what I consider supporting flours. I love **rye flour** for it's rustic color and subtle sweetness and **quinoa flour** for its nutritional profile and grassiness. I love to experiment with homemade multigrain flour blends. For example, I use **oat flour**, rye flour, and whole wheat pastry flour in my Multigrain Pancakes (page 31).

SWEETENERS I've come across dozens of sweeteners produced by small producers over the past few years. The thing I find striking is how no two are alike. The Japanese rock sugar I found in Tokyo couldn't be more different from the golden-hued natural cane sugar I use regularly, which is moist with heavy notes of vanilla and molasses. The Pohutukawa honey I tasted in New Zealand is an entirely different beast from the dark, smoky mango blossom honey Big Tree Farms harvests in Java. I keep a rotation of various sugars, honeys, and syrups on hand, preferring the ones that are minimally refined. Compared to white sugar, their flavor profiles are more interesting, and they can impart a depth and complexity to a recipe you can't get otherwise. In my sweetener collection right now is a number of **honeys, brown rice syrup,** a few bottles of **maple syrup,** numerous natural **cane sugars,** and **unsulphured molasses.**

There is a huge variety of granulated sugars available. They cover the color spectrum from blinding white to deep coffee brown. Broadly speaking, white sugars are more processed than dark—although there are certainly highly processed "false" brown sugars out there. Because there isn't much standardization with regard to labeling, finding a whole sugar can be confusing. Look for words like *unrefined, raw, natural,* and *whole;* seek out a fine grain (comparable to standard white or brown sugar); and opt for dark over light when it comes to color. I've listed a few of my favorite brands in the Sources section (page 235).

The least processed and most whole granulated cane sugar available is dehydrated cane juice, but it often has an irregular consistency and dryness that keeps me from using it more often. My favorite substitute for white sugar is **fine-grain natural cane sugar,** a minimally processed, fragrant, "real" brown sugar that tastes of vanilla with a deep kiss of molasses. I call for it in a number of the recipes in this book.

If you are having a hard time finding a comparable dark brown sugar, you can substitute any light brown sugar or light muscovado sugar in these recipes. Just be sure to buy a fine-grain sugar and sift out any lumps. There are also lots of fine-grain white sugars available that are labeled as natural cane sugar. These won't break the recipes, but they won't give you the exact results you are after, either. If you buy white sugar, look for a sustainably produced organic variety; there are a number that are widely distributed now.

NOODLES AND PASTA I pick up a variety of dried noodles when I'm out and about. I use buckwheat-based **soba noodles** quite often, and beyond that, a variety of Italian pastas. Tiny, rice-shaped **whole wheat orzo** is fun. If you don't think using 100 percent whole wheat pasta is going to fly with your family, try a 50/50 blend of regular and whole grain pasta for starters. It takes a bit of experimenting to find brands of whole grain noodles that aren't overly heavy or texturally "off." Despite labeling, some noodles are made with 100 percent whole grain flours; others are blends of whole grain flours and wheat flour (not whole wheat flour). Make a note of the ones you like, and then taste your way through that family of noodles. You'll get a sense over time of where on the whole grain noodle spectrum you like to be.

LENTILS, SPLIT PEAS, AND THE LITTLEST BEANS I keep my pantry well stocked with a variety of lentils and split peas. They are relatively quick cooking, nutritious, protein-packed, and perfect for use in soups, stews, veggie burgers, dips, and salads. I have a particular fondness for **yellow split peas, tiny black Beluga lentils, lentils du Puy,** and green split peas. All of these are pretty good about holding their shape as long as you don't overcook them. I'm also going to throw **mung beans** in here. I use them quite a lot; and unlike the heirloom beans I talk about on page 11, there is no need to soak them before cooking. Affordable, filling, bulging with protein, they provide a great backbone to any number of meals.

I store each type of dried pulse or bean in a separate large glass Weck jar so I can see when I need to replenish the supply. Be sure to carefully pick over any lentils, beans, or grains before using them—little pebbles and dirt clots often can be found.

DRIED BEANS A quick glance in the cupboard directly to the right of my stove reveals bags of dried beans—lots of them: **baby garbanzos, Christmas limas, flageolets, Sangre de Toro, Rosa de Castilla,** and **runner cannellini** to name a few. Roughly once a week I'll put a pound of them in a large water-filled pot to soak overnight. When I have time the following day, I cook them while I'm doing other things around the house. The specifics are outlined on page 215. It couldn't be simpler.

I like to get to know each individual type of bean, and when I'm trying a new one, I prepare it simply so I can acquaint myself with its unique flavor, texture, and personality. This helps me develop a sense of what I might do the next time to highlight the uniqueness of the bean. Some beans are thin-skinned, some are thick, some lend themselves to a pureed soup, while some are better whole. Or, as I mentioned in *Super Natural Cooking*, one bean might pair with an assertive broth or sauce, while another might be perfect on its own with a drizzling of olive oil and a dusting of grated cheese. I drain and freeze leftover beans, flat, in a plastic freezer bag once they've cooled. They can go straight from the freezer into a hot pan on a whim.

NUTS AND SEEDS A peek into the nuts and seed drawer in my refrigerator uncovers **walnuts, hazelnuts, pepitas, sunflower seeds, pecans, poppy seeds, Marcona and regular almonds, pine nuts,** and both **white and black sesame seeds.** The flavors, the crunch factor, the uses are endless. I like to use them whole, chopped, pureed with other ingredients into sauces, or ground into nut flours for baking.

SPICES, SPICE BLENDS, AND MUSTARDS My spice drawer is the one section of my kitchen I'm powerless to keep under control. I keep a mad collection of **curry powders** and **spice blends** from various travels, as well as little jars of single herbs and spices. People always ask me if I have a favorite curry powder or brand, and the short answer is, there are many I like, but I'm loyal to none. Part of the fun is tasting through spices and various spice combinations, making note of what you like best.

While I like to make **curry pastes** from scratch on occasion, I also keep a variety of **curry pastes** in the refrigerator. They come in handy not only for on-the-fly curry pots, but also for boosts of flavor in everything from frittatas and scrambled eggs to asparagus or potato soup.

Edging out the curry pastes are the **mustards,** mainly Dijon-style mustards—some I make (see page 209), others I buy. You'll see both smooth and grainy mustards get a lot of play in the recipes in this book.

SALT AND PEPPER You'll likely notice I don't automatically season every one of my recipes with salt and pepper. Occasionally, the black pepper is missing. I like black pepper in some preparations, particularly in egg dishes or as a way to counterbalance a savory-sweet sauce—for example in the Black Pepper Tempeh (page 141). But other times I find it can be overpowering, and sometimes even harsh. I tend to prefer **red pepper flakes** or **red chile powders** in much, but not all, of my cooking. When you do use black pepper, be sure to freshly grind it.

SOY SAUCE, SHOYU, AND TAMARI Each of these ingredients brings rich, salty depth and umami to food. While much of the soy sauce you find in the United States is Chinese, I've come to enjoy Japanese variations of soy sauces, also known as shoyu. Shoyu is often more full-bodied than its Chinese counterparts, with a hint of sweetness. Tamari, another type of Japanese soy sauce worth seeking out, is more similar to Chinese soy sauce than shoyu. And wheat-free versions of tamari are available for people with wheat allergies.

Whether you are using shoyu, tamari, or soy sauce, look for naturally fermented versions made from whole ingredients using traditional methods. Chemically processed, fast-tracked soy sauce, often produced in a single day, is a harsh-tasting distant relative to the real thing.

INGREDIENTS IN CANS I always have cans of **coconut milk** on hand—rich, luscious, full-bodied, and flavorful. It's an incredibly versatile ingredient I use when I want all those aforementioned qualities to carry over into a soup, curry, or something I'm baking. It's also a great ingredient to explore if you (or those you're cooking for) follow a vegan or dairy-free diet. The other canned good I keep close at hand is **crushed tomatoes**. It's good in certain curries, Italian sauces, tart fillings, and quick soups.

DAIRY I keep plenty of plain, unsweetened, full-fat **yogurt** in the refrigerator—both regular and Greek style. I cook, bake, and make toppings with it. There is typically a small container of milk around, some homemade crème fraîche (see page 226), my favorite locally produced **cottage cheese**, and a rotating cast of **hard cheeses** like Parmesan or pecorino.

TEMPEH, TOFU, AND SEITAN Not that these three ingredients are the same thing, but I actually group them together in my mind. They all pack a generous protein punch, have the ability to bulk out a meal, and can help turn a side dish into a main dish when appropriate. Each has rich cultural significance and has long been part of the foodways of various Asian cultures. I try not to think of them as meat substitutes, and instead attempt to understand each as an ingredient on its own terms. All three can be cooked using a variety of techniques—sautéing, grilling, baking, steaming. And by experimenting with the form of the ingredient—crumbled, sliced, cubed, diced, grated—you have a broad palette to explore. Both tempeh and tofu take well to assertive marinades.

As far as purchasing goes, I look for the simplest versions—those produced with organic ingredients, without added flavorings and GMOs, that aren't fried, etc. It's worth noting, many tempehs are sold steamed now, cutting out the extra step called for in many older tempeh recipes.

EGGS I eat an egg or two most days and am happy to pay a premium for good ones.

I love to use eggs from local farmers who allow their hens to roam around. The yolks are electric yellow, the flavor richer, and they're known to be more nutritious and lower in cholesterol. The drawback? Fresh eggs are difficult to peel. Any eggs I know I'm going to use for egg salad, I set aside for a few days—I shoot for a week, but they rarely last that long.

VEGETABLE BROTH Truth be told, I rarely make my own broth anymore. I will make it for certain broth-centric soups, or for those times when I'm after a very specific flavor profile, but I don't often make big pots of broth to freeze for later use. My guess is that many of you don't either. Instead, I keep a few boxes of **all-natural vegetable bouillon cubes** on hand, and unapologetically love them. I'm quite partial to the Rapunzel brand vegetable bouillon with sea salt—it dissolves into a clean, bright, herby green vegetable broth that complements many of the other ingredients I use. I use the salted version at about half strength—one cube to 4 or 5 cups / 1 to 1.2 liters of water—to control the salt levels in my recipes. There is also a version without salt, which allows you to completely control how much salt you're using.

You may not be able to get that particular brand where you live, but I'd encourage you to seek out one you do like. The other option, beyond making your own broth or using bouillon, is buying broth that comes in a can or carton. I have yet to find one that I like, and much prefer to use water. Water is completely fine in many cases, and it gives you the latitude to season a dish to your liking later in the cooking process. If you use a bad-tasting broth, you are going to have a hard time getting rid of any off flavors.

CHOCOLATE I rarely purchase chocolate chips anymore; I much prefer to hand-chop or shave bars of chocolate for use in cookies and cakes. I also use a good amount of **nonalkalized cacao powder** and good-quality **semisweet and bittersweet chocolates** when baking.

My Everyday Kitchen

My kitchen spans six paces in one direction and four in the other. There is ample counter space and a refrigerator recessed into a deep alcove in the wall. When I stand at the stove, a door to my right opens onto a small porch, and on occasion the cat from upstairs will come down to visit, or a flashy, green-backed hummingbird will do a quick ballet in the doorway.

I do my best to keep a relatively minimalist kitchen, treating it more like a studio space than anything else, I suppose. I try to keep the counters clear and store ingredients in see-through containers in each cupboard so I can view, at a glance, what I have to work with.

Old often wins out over new in this realm, and most of my bowls, plates, and platters have been chosen at flea markets and yard sales. My flour sifter, food processor, wooden spoons, and pressure cooker are all hand-me-downs from my dad. There is something deeply satisfying to me in using baking sheets coated with a dark patina derived from hundreds of batches of cookies, or cradling a bowl older than I am in the crook of my arm when making a cake batter.

I nearly always choose glass over plastic and keep a large supply of mason and Weck jars on hand to store everything from lentils, flours, and rices to sauces, vinaigrettes, and leftovers. Buying things one piece at a time, each with a story of its own, is a great way to stock a kitchen.

Though this is not intended to be an all-inclusive discussion, I thought it might be helpful if I outlined some of the kitchen equipment I can't imagine doing without.

POTS AND PANS Many people buy their **pots and pans** in sets. In the past, I've found I end up favoring one piece in the set and relegate the others to the back of a cupboard. Now I prefer to invest in good-quality, single pieces and have long since given away all of the pots and pans I was rarely using. Here's what I have (and use) now.

My 11-inch (28cm) oven-safe **stainless steel skillet** with lid is great for making everything from caramelized onions and frittatas to stir-fries and sautés. An extra-large (7¼-quart) **Le Creuset casserole** (Dutch oven) is great for soups and curries, cooking beans or rice, and baking casseroles. I use it on my stovetop and in the oven. A large **pasta pot/stockpot** takes up a lot of space, and I would get rid of it if it weren't so useful, not only for making pasta, but also for boiling and steaming vegetables. It's quite a bit deeper than the casserole. My **small saucepan** (2 quarts) spends most of its working hours heating water for tea, but beyond that, I use it on occasion to heat broth or make sauce. Or, if I need to rig up a double boiler to melt chocolate, I'll use it as the base.

I've done my best to phase out as much nonstick and plastic out of my kitchen as possible, in part because I'm concerned about increased exposure to chemicals leaching from those materials into my food. I prefer to use stainless steel, cast iron, or enameled cast iron instead.

KNIVES, SPOONS, AND SPATULAS I use an Aritsugu brand **santoku knife,** which I bought while traveling through Kyoto, Japan. It's the most serious culinary tool I own, and while it might sound odd, I find myself striving to cook well enough to honor this particular knife. It pains me at times because it isn't stainless steel, so if I even glance at it wrong, it starts to rust. But it holds an edge longer than any other knife I've owned, and the blade makes quick work out of whatever I put beneath it. Aside from that, I use a serrated knife to cut bread. I keep a few **chef's knives** on hand for when there are guest cooks in the kitchen. And related to knives, a **cutting board** that's not too big and not too small is key. Too big, it is unwieldy to wash; too small, things are always tumbling off the sides. My 12 by 16-inch (30 by 40cm) wooden cutting board suits me nicely.

Like many cooks, I have favorite battle-scarred **wooden spoons,** each nick and burn with a story to tell. I also get a lot of use out of a **flat-edged wooden spatula**. It allows me to scrape across a large surface area when I'm stirring risottos or curries, helping me to insure nothing gets stuck to the bottom. It is also kind to my cast-iron pan. Alternatively, I use a strong, flat-edged **metal spatula** for much of my stainless steel skillet work; it allows me to scrape all those browned crispy bits of flavor off the bottom of the pan. I reach for a **rubber spatula** quite often, too—to get the last of a batter out of a mixing bowl, or to empty the last drops of soup into a jar to enjoy at a later time.

APPLIANCES As far as appliances go, there are a small number that make my time in the kitchen more pleasurable. First in line is an **immersion blender**; it makes quick work of pureeing soups. I use my standard blender so infrequently now that I moved it to the garage. I use an **electric stand mixer** to whip egg whites and mix certain doughs. Then I have an ancient **food processor** for making certain pastes, purees, and tart dough.

BAKEWARE I probably have more **cake and tart pans** than I need—cookie cutters, too. I seem to pick them up wherever I go, and when I travel. As far as the pans go, I have them in standard sizes, but because I like to serve cakes, breads, and tarts in their baking pans, I'm always on the lookout for ones that can do the job but that also have a certain amount of visual appeal—perhaps an offbeat shape or interesting patina.

I keep **rimmed** and **unrimmed baking sheets** on hand. The rimmed sheets come in handy when you are roasting an ingredient that gives off liquid; the walled edges prevent the liquid from running onto the floor of the oven. I occasionally place rimmed sheets below items in the oven if I'm at all nervous about the possibility of an overflow. I line baking sheets with **unbleached parchment paper** when I'm concerned about sticking, and have a simple **cooling rack** I use with cookies, muffins, biscuits, and the like when they come out of the oven.

FAVORITE TOOLS There is nothing more helpful than a **kitchen scale** to make quick work of baking projects. It's much quicker (and more accurate, particularly when baking) to weigh ingredients than measure by volume.

I use a small, heavy **mortar and pestle** to grind spices, crush salt, mash garlic, and to make various pastes.

I use my **Microplane grater** to shave chocolate, cheese, ginger, and a variety of fruits and vegetables.

I wish my **salad spinner** took up less space. It's quite greedy in that regard; but when I need it, I really need it. Waterlogged lettuce will repel any oil-based dressing, resulting in puddles on plates instead of well-dressed salad greens. I occasionally use the spinner to dry herbs, spin the water off vegetables before roasting them in the oven, or spin extra moisture off beans or grains if I plan to freeze them.

Relegated to the straggler category, I love my **cast-iron skillet**, the 13-inch-wide professional **crepe machine** Wayne gave me for my birthday years ago, and the Simac **gelato maker** my dad bought on eBay a few years back. I have a **mandoline** that makes slicing paper-thin vegetables a breeze, and **Japanese-style lunch boxes** with reusable, multicompartment containers. They're great for picnics because they allow you to keep components separate until the last minute. But truth be told, none of these get everyday use.

GLASSWARE AND PLATTERS While I'm not sure they count as culinary equipment, I appreciate nice **wine glasses**, so I keep a supply of those on hand with a range of sizes and shapes: flutes, white wine glasses, red wine glasses, or everyday table glasses. They don't necessarily need to be fancy or expensive, just thoughtfully chosen. Opt for clear glass, not cloudy. Narrow silhouettes are for bubbles, and glasses with extra volume are nice so you can swirl your whites and reds. Aside from the practical aspects, some glasses just fit better than others in the hand. Some are tall, stretching for the ceiling; others huddle low and close to the table. These are all considerations that are more of a personal preference than anything else.

And finally, I keep a mishmash of **mixing bowls** and **serving platters** on hand; you can see a range of them in the photos in this book. Most are some shade of off-white. And come to think of it, quite a number of them have some sort of detail or pattern adorning them. I often plate food family style, and always scan my stacks of plates and platters for just the right one. I look for vessels with the appropriate size, shape, and personality. That means pieces that are not too big and not too small, with details that compliment the colors and textures of the ingredients. The right plate can make the food you've prepared look beautiful without requiring much extra effort on your part.

A Few Guidelines

Much of my culinary success (or failure) is connected to decisions I make before entering the kitchen. The single most important variable is finding great ingredients with which to start. This doesn't necessarily mean expensive, it just means great. Look for fresh, bright, vibrant ingredients and go from there. If you know you're likely to find beautiful asparagus on your next shopping run, plan for that, but don't be afraid to mix things up a bit if it's the baby carrots that catch your eye.

I look for fruits and vegetables that have "the glow"—you'll know it when you see it. I know it sounds a bit precious, but it's not. It's simply the combination of good color, texture, and the sense that the ingredient was well tended and very recently picked. I see that glow in swatches of wildflowers when we go hiking sometimes—lively, at attention, proud. That's what I look for in the foods that I buy. I'll have a taste to confirm the flavor, and then go about building a meal (or meals) around it.

Simply put, if you cook with in-season ingredients, preferably locally grown, and seek out ones marked organic—or, at the very least, avoid those that have been grown "conventionally" with lots of herbicides, fungicides, and insecticides—you'll be well on your way to a great meal. And, as you'll see once you get into the recipes, many of them are easily adapted to whatever is available and looks best at your local market. Buy the best ingredients you can afford, and start there.

Another tip, and I know this sounds obvious, be mindful of the weather. A hot, hearty soup on a sweltering day is the culinary equivalent of pulling on wool socks and a heavy coat. Opt for something lighter and cooler. On a cold day, you'll likely crave just the opposite.

USE YOUR SENSES Cooking is not just about taste buds. I try to put all my senses to work throughout the culinary process, whether I'm shopping for peaches or baking a tart. Your eyes will see the moldy berries in a basket; your ears will hear the violent pops and hisses when you add ingredients to overheated oil in a skillet; your nose will smell the rich, nutty scent of butter as it begins to brown; and your fingertips will feel the soft, moist centers of muffins that need more baking time.

TRUST YOURSELF While I've done my best to give you accurate cooking times and ingredient measurements with this collection of recipes, in the end, the recipes are written to my tastes, not yours. Don't follow them blindly. If you're roasting cherry tomatoes in the oven and you feel a few extra minutes will do them some good, go for it. If you like a spicier curry sauce, feel free to add more curry paste. If you like your salad dressing with a bit more edge, add more lemon juice or vinegar, one splash at a time. Even the best recipe writers are using different produce and ingredients than you, different pans, a different oven—just about every element in cooking is variable. It's the nature of the beast. As I've become a better cook over the years, I've learned a lot. The most valuable lesson? Trust my own instincts, trust my own taste buds. With cooking, like any other skill, you learn by doing, with your instincts growing sharper and more refined over time.

ADAPT Many of the recipes in this book are seasonally adaptable. That means if I happen to use huckleberries in a recipe, but blackberries are in season at your local market, they would likely make a reasonable substitute. If I call for winter squash, and you have sweet potatoes on hand, consider using them instead.

The one place I would encourage you to be more conservative with substitutions is when it comes to baking—trading one flour for another or cutting back on one ingredient and increasing another can yield disappointing results. In many of the recipes, I call out favorite substitutions, ones that I know work well.

CHECK YOUR OVEN TEMPERATURE If you've been frustrated by baking in the past, you might want to check the accuracy of your oven. You can purchase a simple, freestanding oven thermometer for a few dollars. You'll know exactly how hot your oven is; and if your oven is consistently running hot or cold, you can have it adjusted.

USE FRESH BAKING POWDER AND BAKING SODA For successful baking, second in importance to checking your oven temperature is making sure your baking powder and soda aren't past their prime. Replace them regularly, roughly every 6 months. To see if your baking powder or baking soda is still active, add lemon juice to a little baking soda or hot water to a spoonful of baking powder. If they bubble and fizz, you're in good shape. Also, look for aluminum-free baking powder to avoid ingesting aluminum and side-step that metallic taste that some baking powders impart.

USE YOUR FREEZER I've started to use my freezer more enthusiastically in the past few years. I freeze all sorts of seasonal fruits, soups, cooked beans, tart shells, cooked grains, and doughs. It can be one of your strongest allies when it comes time to turn out a great-tasting, last-minute meal in a reasonable amount of time.

MEASURE FLOURS CAREFULLY When I call for flour in a recipe, it means measured without first sifting. Spoon the flour into the measuring cup until it heaps above the rim. Resist the urge to tap it or thwack it on the counter—you don't want to compact the flour. Sweep a straightedge across the top of the cup to level the flour. If your flour has been compacted at the base of the bag or canister, be sure to fluff it up a bit before measuring.

BREAKFAST

breakfast

ON A CLEAR DAY, the morning sun greets me at the back of the house. It creeps up from the east and clears the peach-colored, pitched-roof Victorian across the back fence. Then, working its way over the tall eugenia trees, it begins to send warm bands of sunlight through our wood-framed windows into the kitchen. I like to sit there on a stool, sunbeams at my back, espresso in hand.

I decided years back to start eating a "real breakfast." It wasn't something I was in the habit of doing. Some days a real breakfast means a bit of homemade granola and yogurt, other days it means turning on the oven for a batch of fresh-baked biscuits or a family-style frittata. Some days I have time to sit and linger, other days are more hurried. Either way, I try to enjoy something substantial.

I tend to lean toward a savory breakfast, but you'll find a handful of tried-and-true, sweet-tinged favorites in this chapter as well.

Muesli | 25
oats, golden raisins, marcona almonds

Granola | 26
currants, walnuts, orange zest

Oatmeal | 29
prunes, hazelnuts, brown butter, yogurt

Multigrain Pancakes | 31
whole grain flours & buttermilk

Spinach Strata | 33
whole grain bread, mustard, feta, oregano

Fruit Salad | 34
apples, raspberries, grapes, figs, peaches

Sun Toast | 36
whole wheat seed bread & fresh eggs

Lemon-Zested Bulgur Wheat | 37
coconut milk, toasted almonds, poppy seeds

Millet Muffins | 41
raw millet & honey

Yogurt Biscuits | 42
spelt flour & greek-style yogurt

Baked Oatmeal | 44
oats, huckleberries, walnuts

Bran Muffins | 47
whole wheat pastry flour, buttermilk, maple syrup

Crepes | 50
rye flour & sea salt

Frittata | 53
seasonal produce, shallots, goat cheese

Flecked with chopped Marcona almonds and golden raisins, this muesli is something I make a batch of every week or so. The dry ingredients fit perfectly in a quart-size mason jar, and the night before I want a bowl, I simply stir a scoop into a bowl of thinned-out yogurt and let it sit overnight in the refrigerator.

Muesli

OATS, GOLDEN RAISINS, MARCONA ALMONDS

In a large bowl, toss together the oats, almonds, raisins, wheat germ, and salt. Transfer to a quart-size mason jar (or equivalent) until you are ready to use it.

For each serving, spoon 1/2 cup / 4 oz / 115 g yogurt into a bowl, thin with 1/4 cup / 60 ml water, and sweeten with a splash of maple syrup. Stir in 1/2 cup / 2 oz / 60 g of the muesli and let sit in the refrigerator for at least an hour, or preferably overnight. Top with a small handful of raisins and serve

SERVES 6 TO 8

3 cups / 10.5 oz / 300 g rolled oats

1/2 cup / 2 oz / 60 g chopped Marcona almonds

1/4 cup / 1 oz / 30 g golden raisins, plus more to serve

1/4 cup / .5 oz / 15 g raw wheat or oat germ

1/4 teaspoon fine-grain sea salt

Plain yogurt, to serve

Water, to serve

Maple syrup, to serve (optional)

Nutty, orange-scented, and peppered with tiny currants, this has become our house granola. On occasion, I do a more decadent "weekend" version with double the butter and a bit more maple syrup.

Granola

CURRANTS, WALNUTS, ORANGE ZEST

4 cups / 14 oz / 400 g rolled oats

1½ cups / 6 oz / 170 g walnut halves

1 cup / 2 oz / 60 g unsweetened shredded large-flake coconut

½ teaspoon fine-grain sea salt

⅔ cup / 3 oz / 85 g dried currants

Grated zest of 2 oranges

⅓ cup / 3 oz / 85 g unsalted butter

½ cup / 120 ml maple syrup

Preheat the oven to 300°F / 150°C with racks in the top and bottom thirds of the oven. Set out two rimmed baking sheets.

Combine the oats, walnuts, coconut, salt, currants, and orange zest in a large mixing bowl. Heat the butter in a small saucepan over low heat and stir in the maple syrup. Whisk until thoroughly combined, then pour the maple mixture over the oat mixture and stir until everything is well coated, at least 30 seconds. Divide the mixture equally between the two baking sheets and spread into a thin layer.

Bake, stirring a couple times along the way, for 40 to 50 minutes, or until the granola is toasty and deeply golden. You may want to rotate the pans once, top to bottom, to ensure even baking.

Remove from the oven and press down on the granola with a metal spatula—you'll get more clumps this way. Let cool completely, then store in an airtight container at room temperature.

MAKES ABOUT 8 CUPS / 32 OZ / 910 G

As much as I love chunky, hearty steel-cut oats and long, lazy breakfasts, there are mornings when I don't have extra minutes to spare. Enter old-fashioned rolled oats. A pot comes together in about 10 minutes, simmering away while I get dressed. You'll make a cranky mess of the pan, but you can simply let it soak while you're out. Any cooked-on oats will wipe off later in the day with little effort.

Swirling a bit of plain yogurt, cream, or (even better) crème fraîche into each bowl of cooked oats before eating helps emphasize the oatmeal's creaminess. And when it comes to toppings, the combination of toasted hazelnuts, prunes, and brown butter is hard to beat, although some days I just enjoy the oatmeal straight with a sprinkling of muscovado sugar. Be sure to use rolled oats here, and not instant oats.

Oatmeal

PRUNES, HAZELNUTS, BROWN BUTTER & YOGURT

Bring the water to a boil in a small saucepan. Stir in the oats and salt. Turn down the heat and simmer until the oatmeal has thickened and the oats are tender, about 10 minutes. Remove from heat and fold in the yogurt and most of the prunes. Taste. Add maple syrup if you like a bit of sweetness and sweeten to your liking.

Divide the oatmeal into four small bowls and top with the remaining prunes, the hazelnuts, and the tiniest drizzle of brown butter.

SERVES 4

3 cups / 700 ml water

1½ cups / 5 oz / 140 g rolled oats

½ teaspoon fine-grain sea salt

¼ cup / 2 oz / 60 g plain yogurt, cream, or crème fraîche (see page 226)

8 prunes, chopped

2 tablespoons maple syrup, or to taste

20 hazelnuts, toasted (see page 219) and chopped

Drizzle of brown butter (see page 225)

OTHER INGREDIENTS I LIKE TO FOLD INTO THE BATTER:

- 2 tablespoons poppy seeds or a handful of finely chopped toasted walnuts or pecans
- A splash of pure vanilla extract with lots of chopped hulled strawberries
- Grated zest of one lemon and a handful of toasted sunflower seeds

You might imagine a pancake made from 100 percent whole grain flours would be dense and heavy. Not so. Light, golden, and moist, with enough buttermilk to give a bit of tang, these pancakes are perfect on a Saturday morning. And, as a bonus, the leftover batter keeps for days. Little silver-dollar pancakes are my shape of choice here, but you can certainly go larger. To switch things up, you can use the batter in a waffle iron as well. If you don't have natural cane sugar on hand, substitute whatever brown sugar you do have.

Multigrain Pancakes

WHOLE GRAIN FLOURS & BUTTERMILK

Combine the flours, sugar, baking powder, and salt in a large mixing bowl. In a separate medium bowl, whisk together the buttermilk and eggs, add the butter, and whisk again.

Heat a griddle or skillet until medium-hot, brush with a bit of butter, and test the temperature. If a drop of water dances across the surface, you're in the ballpark. When you're ready to make the pancakes, pour the wet ingredients over the dry, and stir until just combined.

If you're cooking silver-dollar pancakes, pour the batter 2 tablespoons at a time into small puddles on the griddle. Keep in mind they spread a bit. If you want larger pancakes, pour the batter 1/4 to 1/3 cup at a time onto the griddle. Cook until the bottoms are deep golden in color and the tops have set a bit, then use a spatula to flip the pancakes and cook the other sides until golden and the pancakes are cooked through. Repeat with the remaining batter. Serve warm topped with butter, Blackberry-Maple Compote (page 212), or your favorite syrup.

MAKES 24 TO 26 SILVER-DOLLAR PANCAKES
OR 12 LARGE PANCAKES

1 cup / 4.5 oz / 125 g whole wheat pastry flour

1/2 cup / 1.5 oz / 45 g oat flour

1/2 cup / 2 oz / 60 g rye flour

1 1/2 tablespoons natural cane sugar

1 tablespoon aluminum-free baking powder

Scant 1/2 teaspoon fine-grain sea salt

2 cups / 475 ml buttermilk

3 large eggs, lightly beaten

1/3 cup / 3 oz / 85 g butter, melted and cooled a bit, plus more for the skillet

You put together everything for this strata the night before you want to serve it, then bake it the next morning. Eggs, whole wheat bread, chopped spinach, and a bit of cheese make it substantial, but not overly indulgent. A couple tips: leave the crust on the bread, it makes for a rustic strata with more structure. And, if you don't have day-old bread, you can dry fresh bread in a 250°F / 120°C oven for 10 to 15 minutes, letting it cool before using. I often make the strata with leftover Rye Soda Bread (page 96), but any dense, brown, or whole grain bread will do.

Spinach Strata

WHOLE GRAIN BREAD, MUSTARD, FETA, OREGANO

Rub a splash of olive oil in a 9-inch / 23cm square baking dish (or equivalent). Alternatively, line it with parchment paper. Sprinkle the baking dish or parchment paper with lemon zest and set aside.

In a medium bowl, whisk the olive oil, mustard, salt, and pepper with a splash of the milk. Whisk in the rest of the milk and the eggs.

Put the bread in the prepared baking dish and top with the spinach and half of the feta. Gently toss with your hands—just enough that the spinach and cheese mixes with all those pieces of bread. Make sure the bread is relatively level in the baking dish. Very slowly drizzle the egg mixture over the bread and sprinkle with the remaining feta. Cover and refrigerate overnight.

The next morning, when you are ready to bake the strata, preheat the oven to 350°F / 175°C with a rack in the top third of the oven.

Bake the strata, uncovered, for 45 to 55 minutes, until the egg is set in the middle and the edges are browned. You need to cut into it a bit to be sure it is well cooked, particularly in the center. It can be a bit tricky to tell; err on the side of overdone versus underdone. I like to brown the top a bit more under the broiler (low setting) before removing the strata from the oven, but it's an optional extra step. Skip this step if you've lined your pan with parchment paper. Serve warm, drizzled with a bit of olive oil and sprinkled with the fresh oregano.

Grated zest of 1 lemon

2 tablespoons extra-virgin olive oil, plus more for drizzling

2 teaspoons Dijon-style mustard

1/2 teaspoon fine-grain sea salt

1/4 teaspoon freshly ground black pepper

2 cups / 475 ml milk

6 large eggs

3 cups / 8 oz / 225 g day-old 1/2-inch / 1cm whole wheat bread cubes

2 cups / 3 oz / 85 g finely chopped baby spinach

1/2 cup / 2.5 oz / 70 g feta cheese, crumbled

1 teaspoon fresh oregano leaves, chopped

SERVES 6

My friend Jennifer Jeffrey made this jewel-toned beauty of a fruit salad as part of a breakfast we had while on a weekend getaway to Lake Tahoe. It was early fall and the range of colors in the fruit she used was vibrant and stunning— sunset-streaked nectarines alongside raspberries a shade of deep pink reserved for only the juiciest of lip glosses. Use whatever fruit is in season where you live, and the most flavorful you can find. If you pre-cut the apples or pears, keep them in a mild lemon water (5 cups / 1.2 liters of water mixed with the juice of one lemon) so they don't brown. Then drain well before using.

Fruit Salad

APPLES, RASPBERRIES, GRAPES, FIGS, PEACHES

1 cup / 5 oz / 140 g
  raspberries, cut in half
2 cups / 10 oz / 280 g
  seedless grapes, whole or
  cut in half
6 small fresh figs, quartered
2 small apples or pears, cored
  and cut into 1-inch / 2.5cm
  pieces
1 large nectarine, pitted and
  cut into 1-inch / 2.5cm
  pieces
Big squeeze of fresh orange
  juice
1 tablespoon chopped fresh
  mint, chopped (optional)
Drizzle of honey

Just before serving, combine the raspberries, grapes, figs, apples, and nectarine in a large bowl. Add the orange juice, mint, and honey. Toss very gently. The last thing you want is for the fruit to get banged up and mushy. Serve immediately.

SERVES 4 TO 6

This breakfast is all about the crunch of buttery toast playing off a single, delicate egg cooked in the bread's center. I call it sun toast, but you might recognize it by one of its other names: egg in a hole, bull's-eye, egg on a raft, or, for the more literal-minded, framed egg.

Sun Toast

WHOLE WHEAT SEED BREAD & FRESH EGGS

1-inch / 2.5cm thick slice artisan whole wheat seed bread

1 large egg

Slather of unsalted butter

1 clove garlic, peeled

Use a 1½-inch / 4cm round cookie cutter to cut a circle out of the middle of the piece of bread. You'll use both pieces, so don't throw the little circle away. Butter the bread and the circle on both sides.

Place the bread pieces in a large skillet over medium-low heat. Toast both sides of each but don't let them get too dark at this point. You don't want the butter to smoke or the bread to burn. Once toasted, carefully crack the egg into the hole in the bread and let it cook until the egg white sets and looks about halfway done. Use a spatula to flip and cook the other side until deeply golden, a few minutes all told. The little round piece might be done more quickly; if so, just remove it from the pan. Do your best to avoid scorching the egg, but cook it to your liking—less time if you like it on the runny side, more if you like it set.

Place everything on a plate and rub a clove of garlic along the surface of the bread. I like to make these to order, one at a time, served alongside a pitcher of hot French press coffee.

SERVES 1

There are a few secrets to share here. For starters, seek out a loaf of unsliced artisan bread, and use the best eggs you can get your hands on. I buy a whole wheat seed bread from a local bakery, but your favorite loaf will work just as well. A mostly straight-sided bread and a slice cut from its center is most desirable. As far as technique goes, you are trying to get the toast deeply golden without scorching or overcooking the eggs. Be mindful of the thickness of your toast, as well as the size of hole you cut from the center. Too thick a slice or too big a hole and the egg won't fill it. Too thin a slice or too small a hole and the egg will overflow. Still tastes good, just not as nice to look at.

Oatmeal lovers should give this a go. Tiny flecks of wheat (bulgur) are simmered in coconut milk until the grains soften and become thick and creamy. Finish things off with a touch of lemon zest, poppy seeds, almonds for crunch, and a kiss of local honey, and you have a nice bowl of hot, toothsome breakfast cereal that should keep you full until lunch.

Lemon-Zested Bulgur Wheat

COCONUT MILK, TOASTED ALMONDS, POPPY SEEDS

In a medium saucepan over medium heat, bring the coconut milk and 3/4 cup / 180ml of the water to a simmer. Stir in the bulgur, bring the mixture just to a boil, then dial down the heat and simmer the mixture, stirring often, for 5 to 20 minutes, or until the bulgur is creamy, but still retains some texture. The size of the bulgur grains will dictate how long they need to cook. If the liquid in the pan is absorbed before the bulgur has fully cooked, stir in more water, 1/4 cup / 60ml at a time, until done. Stir in the poppy seeds, lemon zest, and honey. Serve hot in individual bowls topped with the toasted almonds.

SERVES 4

1 cup / 240 ml coconut milk

About 1 1/2 cups / 355 ml water

1 cup / 5 oz / 140 g fine or medium bulgur

1/2 teaspoon fine-grain sea salt

1 1/2 teaspoons poppy seeds

Grated zest of 1 lemon

1 1/2 tablespoons honey, or to taste

1/3 cup / 1 oz / 30 g sliced almonds, toasted (see page 219)

Bulgur is quick-cooking whole wheat that has been boiled, dried, and ground into various sizes. I use fine- or medium-grain bulgur for this recipe. The finer the bulgur, the quicker it cooks. When I'm short on time, I grab fine-grain, and when I have a bit more time, I grab medium-grain.

These muffins seem to go over particularly well with cornbread lovers. For those of you who use cornbread for croutons, as a stuffing base, or in, say, a cornbread panzanella, you might want to experiment with these muffins as an alternative.

Durable but not dense, sweet but not sugary, crunchy, and just a smidge lemony—this is what my friend Jess Thomson had to say about her millet muffins. It was just enough to convince me to get a batch in the oven. They bake into golden-topped perfection: moist, honey-kissed, and delightfully textured. My two-year-old nephew loves them plain, but I think they're perfect slathered with salted butter and boozy Roasted Strawberries (page 228).

Millet Muffins

RAW MILLET & HONEY

Preheat the oven to 400°F / 205°C with a rack in the top third of the oven. Butter a standard 12-cup muffin pan or line with paper liners.

Whisk together the flour, millet, baking powder, baking soda, and salt in a large bowl. In another bowl, whisk together the yogurt, eggs, butter, honey, and lemon zest and juice until smooth. Add the wet ingredients to the dry ingredients and stir until the flour is just incorporated. Divide the batter among the muffin cups, spooning a heaping 1/4 cup / 60 ml batter into each one, filling it a bit below the rim.

Bake for about 15 minutes, until the muffin tops are browned and just barely beginning to crack. Let cool for 5 minutes in the pan, then turn the muffins out of the pan to cool completely on a wire rack.

MAKES 12 MUFFINS

2 1/4 cups / 10 oz / 280 g whole wheat pastry flour
1/3 cup / 2 oz / 60 g raw millet
1 teaspoon aluminum-free baking powder
1 teaspoon baking soda
1/2 teaspoon fine-grain sea salt
1 cup / 8 oz / 225 g plain yogurt
2 large eggs, lightly beaten
1/2 cup / 120 ml barely melted unsalted butter
1/2 cup / 120 ml honey
Grated zest and 2 tablespoons juice from 1 lemon

There are two techniques I use to make these biscuits great: preheating the baking sheet and stacking and pressing out the dough a few times to create feathery layers. I don't call for two types of flours to be difficult; you can use all spelt or all whole wheat pastry flour, but you'll end up with much denser, wheatier biscuits. If you go that route, you'll want to add a bit more yogurt as well. I call for Greek-style yogurt here, but you can use regular plain yogurt if that's what you keep on hand. And when I have a surplus of crème fraîche (see page 226) to use up, I'll substitute that. It makes the most light, flaky, decadent biscuits you can imagine.

Yogurt Biscuits

SPELT FLOUR & GREEK-STYLE YOGURT

1¼ cups / 5 oz / 140 g spelt flour or whole wheat pastry flour

1¼ cups / 5.5 oz / 155 g unbleached all-purpose flour, plus more if needed

1½ teaspoons fine-grain sea salt

1 tablespoon aluminum-free baking powder

½ cup / 4 oz / 115 g unsalted butter, chilled and cut into tiny cubes

1⅓ cups / 11 oz / 310 g Greek-style yogurt

Preheat the oven to 450°F / 230°C with a rack in the middle of the oven. Place an ungreased baking sheet in the oven to preheat as well.

Combine the flours, salt, and baking powder in a food processor. Sprinkle the butter across the top of the dry ingredients and pulse about 20 times, or until the mixture resembles tiny pebbles on a sandy beach. Add the yogurt and pulse a few times, or until the yogurt is just incorporated. Avoid overmixing; it's fine if there are a few dry patches. Gather the dough into a ball and turn it out onto a lightly floured surface. Knead five times and press into an inch-thick square. Cut in half and stack one on the other. Repeat two more times—flattening and stacking, then cutting. Add more all-purpose flour to prevent sticking when needed. Press or roll out the dough into a ¾-inch / 2cm thick rectangle, but no thicker; if the dough is too tall, the biscuits will tilt and tip over while baking. Cut the dough into twelve equal biscuits.

Transfer the biscuits to the preheated baking sheet leaving ½ inch / 1.5cm between each biscuit. Bake for 15 to 18 minutes, until the bottoms are deeply golden and the biscuits are cooked through. I like to eat them hot, split through the middle, with a touch of butter on each half.

MAKES 12 BISCUITS

AS FAR AS ADD-INS GO, ON OCCASION I'LL PULSE IN:

- A handful of chopped fresh herbs and a bit of grated lemon zest
- A handful of finely chopped sun-dried tomatoes, some crumbled feta, and a few minced olives
- A finely chopped serrano chile, plus a handful of shredded aged artisan Cheddar cheese

I've enjoyed oats a thousand different ways in my life, and this is my favorite. A layer of fruit lines the base of a well-buttered baking dish. The fruit is then topped with a blend of rolled oats, nuts, and spices. A wet mixture of milk, egg, melted butter, and vanilla is drizzled over the dry ingredients before baking to a golden-topped, fruit-scented finish. Be sure to use rolled oats and not instant oats.

Baked Oatmeal

OATS, HUCKLEBERRIES, WALNUTS

2 cups / 7 oz / 200 g rolled oats

1/2 cup / 2 oz / 60 g walnut pieces, toasted (see page 219) and chopped

1/3 cup / 2 oz / 60 g natural cane sugar or maple syrup, plus more for serving

1 teaspoon aluminum-free baking powder

1 1/2 teaspoons ground cinnamon

Scant 1/2 teaspoon fine-grain sea salt

2 cups / 475 ml milk

1 large egg

3 tablespoons unsalted butter, melted and cooled slightly

2 teaspoons pure vanilla extract

2 ripe bananas, cut into 1/2-inch / 1cm pieces

1 1/2 cups / 6.5 oz / 185 g huckleberries, blueberries, or mixed berries

Preheat the oven to 375°F / 190°C with a rack in the top third of the oven. Generously butter the inside of an 8-inch / 20cm square baking dish.

In a bowl, mix together the oats, half the walnuts, the sugar, if using, the baking powder, cinnamon, and salt.

In another bowl, whisk together the maple syrup, if using, the milk, egg, half of the butter, and the vanilla.

Arrange the bananas in a single layer in the bottom of the prepared baking dish. Sprinkle two-thirds of the berries over the top. Cover the fruit with the oat mixture. Slowly drizzle the milk mixture over the oats. Gently give the baking dish a couple thwacks on the countertop to make sure the milk moves through the oats. Scatter the remaining berries and remaining walnuts across the top.

Bake for 35 to 45 minutes, until the top is nicely golden and the oat mixture has set. Remove from the oven and let cool for a few minutes. Drizzle the remaining melted butter on the top and serve. Sprinkle with a bit more sugar or drizzle with maple syrup if you want it a bit sweeter.

SERVES 6 GENEROUSLY, OR 12 AS PART OF A LARGER BRUNCH SPREAD

Although I love this huckleberry version, feel free to substitute your favorite in-season berries, or any other fruit for that matter. Another version I love is made with plump, amaretto-soaked golden raisins in place of the berries and sliced almonds in place of the walnuts.

If you want to mix things up a bit, sprinkle a scant cup of chopped dates or currants into the batter, or the grated zest of a couple lemons or oranges, before baking. Alternatively, I sometimes sprinkle the tops of the muffins with sunflower seeds or finely chopped walnuts before baking.

If good bran muffins have eluded you, give these a shot. After years of tweaks, this has become my basic, go-to bran muffin recipe. It results in a substantial, crunchy muffin top hiding a tender, barely sweet crumb underneath. I think the muffins are best served warm with a smear of salted butter, but I know others who prefer a slather of apricot jam.

The recipe calls for plain, unsweetened bran cereal, although at times I substitute other crunchy, hearty cereals—Ezekiel 4:9 sprouted grain cereal works particularly well. Muscovado sugar makes a nice substitution for the natural cane sugar here.

Bran Muffins

WHOLE WHEAT PASTRY FLOUR, BUTTERMILK, MAPLE SYRUP

Preheat the oven to 400°F / 205°C with a rack in the middle of the oven. Generously butter a standard 12-cup muffin pan.

In a large bowl, whisk together the eggs, buttermilk, melted butter, and maple syrup. Sprinkle the bran and cereal across the top, stir, and allow the mixture to sit for 5 minutes.

In the meantime, in a separate small bowl, whisk together the flour, sugar, baking soda, baking powder, and salt. Sprinkle the dry ingredients over the top of the wet and stir until just combined. Immediately fill each muffin cup three-quarters full.

Bake for 18 to 22 minutes, until the edges of the muffins begin to brown and the tops have set. Let cool for 5 minutes in the pan, then turn the muffins out of the pan to cool completely on a wire rack.

MAKES 12 MUFFINS

2 large eggs, lightly beaten

1 cup / 240 ml buttermilk or plain yogurt

1/2 cup / 120 ml barely melted unsalted butter

1/4 cup / 60 ml maple syrup

1/2 cup / .75 oz / 20 g unprocessed wheat bran or oat bran

1 1/2 cups / 4 oz / 115 g plain, unsweetened bran cereal

1 cup / 4 oz / 115 g whole wheat pastry flour

1/4 cup / 1.25 oz / 35 g natural cane sugar

1 teaspoon baking soda

1 teaspoon aluminum-free baking powder

1 teaspoon fine-grain sea salt

This simple batter makes a family-size batch of rustic rye-flour crepes, which I make quite frequently. A word of advice: aim for a smooth, lump-free batter and (really) resist the urge to skip the straining step. A mesh strainer is the best tool for the job—don't even try cheesecloth (it makes a mess) and making the batter in a blender doesn't yield the same results. I've tested many different approaches to crepes, and broadly speaking, 100 percent whole grain flour blends aren't as good as a mixture of a whole grain flour and all-purpose flour. The former tends to make crepes that are too heavy and flabby, and that take too long to cook, which results in steamed crepes. This particular recipe works well in a pan or with a tabletop crepe maker. You can pre-cook crepes ahead of time if you like. Stack the crepes between sheets of parchment paper, and then reheat in a lightly buttered skillet and fill with toppings when you are ready to eat.

{ pictured on page 48 and 49 }

Crepes

RYE FLOUR & SEA SALT

3/4 cup / 3 oz / 85 g rye flour

1 1/4 cups / 5 oz / 140 g unbleached all-purpose flour

1/2 teaspoon fine-grain sea salt

3 large eggs

2 cups / 475 ml water, plus more if needed

Unsalted butter for cooking

Fillings (see box, page 51)

To make the crepe batter, combine the flours and salt in a bowl. Use a fork to stir in the eggs until the texture becomes raggedy. Gradually stir in the water. The batter may seem a bit thin, but it will thicken as it rests. Remove the lumps from the batter by pushing and smushing all the batter through a not-too-fine wire-mesh strainer using a wooden spoon or rigid spatula. Rest the batter on a countertop for at least 30 minutes, then stir again before using. It should have the consistency of smooth heavy cream. If you need to thin with more water, do so a few tablespoons at a time.

To cook the crepes, heat an 8-inch / 20cm nonstick or well-seasoned skillet over medium heat. Rub with a touch of butter and pour just enough batter into the pan to provide a thin coating; in an 8-inch / 20cm pan, this means about 1/4 cup / 60 ml. As you pour, rotate the pan so the batter runs to cover the entire bottom. If you feel compelled to patch holes, sparingly add dabs of extra batter, but work quickly and try to keep the crepe thin. Cook for a few minutes until the crepe is browned, then flip with a spatula and brown the second side before adding your desired fillings. Re-butter the pan every couple of crepes.

If your batter isn't spreading easily over the pan, it is perfectly fine to thin it with more water. Then try again. It takes a bit of practice. Alternatively, you can use a crepe maker like the one I have, which is a lot of fun, and you can make much larger crepes. Any unused batter keeps well in the refrigerator for a few days.

MAKES ABOUT 12 CREPES

As far as fillings go, the possibilities are endless. My advice? Set up a selection of toppings and resist the urge to overfill. I tend to keep things simple with a sprinkling of grated, aged Gruyère, or whatever cooked seasonal vegetables I have on hand. Thin slices of pan-fried potatoes and a generous slather of pesto or a dash of hot sauce work particularly well. Other times I'll add a beaten egg to the pan and throw a cooked crepe down on top of it. Once the egg is cooked, flip, sprinkle with a bit of cheese, fold in half, and enjoy. On the sweet side, these crepes like berries, a bit of shaved chocolate, or muscovado sugar sprinkled on top and cooked until warmed through or melted.

I make dozens of variations on this recipe, using whatever vegetables are in season. I do one variation where I whisk 2 teaspoons of Thai curry paste into the eggs, and use broccoli as the vegetable. In another version, curry powder is the spicing and cauliflower is the vegetable.

Frittatas. For years I started them on the stovetop, then finished in a hot oven—a perfectly acceptable approach. But it wasn't until I began to finish my frittatas under the broiler that they became exceptional. The eggs puff up and stay light and the toppings brown and crisp perfectly, while the frittata bottom escapes scorching. An added bonus is this approach takes less time.

A 12-inch / 30cm cast-iron skillet is my preferred pan for frittatas, but any ovenproof pan will do. For a smaller crowd, use the same technique but halve the amount of eggs, cheese, and vegetables.

Frittata

SEASONAL PRODUCE, SHALLOTS, GOAT CHEESE

Heat the oil in a heavy ovenproof 12-inch / 30cm skillet over medium-high heat. Stir in the onions, potatoes, half of the shallots, and two big pinches of salt. Cover and cook, stirring occasionally, until the potatoes are just cooked through, about 5 minutes. Stir in the vegetables and cook for another minute or two, until they soften up a bit. Set aside half of this mixture on a plate.

Whisk 1/2 teaspoon salt into the eggs, and pour the eggs into the skillet. Cook over medium-low heat until the eggs are just set and there isn't a lot of liquid in the pan, about 5 minutes. To facilitate this, run a spatula underneath the perimeter of the frittata and tilt the pan so the uncooked eggs run to the underside. The key is to avoid browning on the bottom. Top with the reserved vegetable mixture and sprinkle with the cheese and the remaining shallot.

Place under a broiler (a low setting will give you more control, if you have that option) for a couple minutes, or just until the top of the frittata is puffed up and set. Resist the urge to walk away—the frittata can go from perfect to burned in just a few seconds. Remove from the broiler and let sit for a minute or two. Sprinkle with the chives, drizzle with a bit of olive oil, and serve warm or at room temperature, right out of the pan.

SERVES 8

2 tablespoons extra-virgin olive oil or melted clarified butter (see page 224), plus more for drizzling

2 small onions, chopped

8 ounces / 225 g new potatoes, unpeeled, sliced into paper thin rounds

2 shallots, chopped

Fine-grain sea salt

8 ounces / 225 g seasonal vegetables, such as summer squash, broccoli, or asparagus, cut into 1/2-inch / 1cm pieces

10 large eggs, well beaten

1/4 cup / 1 oz / 30 g crumbled goat or feta cheese

Small bunch of chives, chopped

LUNCH

lunch

I MAKE LUNCH FOR MYSELF MOST DAYS. Sometimes I cook from scratch, other times I compile something from the leftovers of previous meals. Lunch steadies me for the rest of the day and allows me a bit of time to recharge, relax, enjoy myself, and, at times, reflect. It's my opinion that a good lunch doesn't need to be a fancy affair, but it should make an attempt at being proper. Meaning, I like to stop everything and set my sights on enjoying a lunch that's flavorful, nutritious, and thoughtfully prepared.

I most like to eat lunch in places where there is fresh air—near open windows, on rooftops, in backyards, and on porches. Places where you can hear birds chirp or watch clouds swim across the sky. I like to eat lunch alone. I like to eat lunch with friends. I like to eat lunch with my sister, or with Wayne. Quiet lunches are nice and so are chatty lunches, and the lunches that fall somewhere in between.

The beach isn't far from here, and I like to eat lunch there on warm days and cold, with waves crashing straight ahead, pelicans diving deep and putting on a show. Or at one of the nearby parks, picnic blanket unfurled, reclining back into one of San Francisco's sloping greens.

I like to eat lunch perched high on one of the stools in my kitchen, or on nice days, barefoot on the back deck, sitting in the old wood chair that looks out toward the park. Or on the stairs behind Coit Tower, the parrots chattering to each other in the trees and San Francisco at my feet. Sometimes I'm stuck inside, and that's okay, too. Actually, I've found that no matter where I am, or what I'm in the middle of, I can usually find a patch of good light with an interesting view in which to sit down and enjoy a homemade lunch—even if it's reheated soup from last night's dinner.

Open-Face Egg Sandwich | 60
whole grain toast, herbs, yogurt

Tortellini Salad | 61
avocado, sprouts, cilantro, pine nuts

Summer Squash Soup | 62
red thai curry, tofu croutons

Chickpea Wraps | 64
whole wheat lavash, celery, dill, mustard

Mostly Not Potato Salad | 66
dill, leek, celery, mustard, potatoes, tofu

Chickpeas & Dandelion Greens | 69
red pepper flakes & hot olive oil dressing

Whole Grain Rice Salad | 70
spinach, basil, goat cheese, walnuts,
cherry vinaigrette

Shaved Fennel Salad | 72
zucchini coins, feta, pine nuts

Mixed Melon Bowl | 73
mint, lemon juice, feta cheese,
kalamata olives

Ravioli Salad | 75
black olives & pepitas

Yellow Split Peas & Greens | 78
mixed greens, serrano chile,
lemon juice

Panzanella | 79
grilled tofu, sunflower sprouts,
peanut butter, oven-roasted tomatoes

Kale Salad | 80
toasted coconut & sesame oil

Mixed Green Salad | 82
strawberries, parmesan, black pepper,
balsamic vinegar

Black Bean Salad | 83
oven-roasted tomatoes, almonds,
lemon zest, feta

White Beans & Cabbage | 86
parmesan, potatoes, shallots

Broccoli Gribiche | 88
roasted potatoes, red wine vinegar,
capers, mustard

Chanterelle Tacos | 93
serrano chile, garlic, parmesan

Orzo Salad | 95
whole wheat orzo, broccoli pesto, lemon,
avocado, crème fraîche

Rye Soda Bread | 96
rye flour, buttermilk, dill butter

Dill Butter | 99
dill, butter, farmer cheese, chives,
shallots

This bright, simple egg salad served on top of thin, toasted whole grain bread is my sandwich of choice a couple days a week. I run a bit of butter along one side of a slice of hot toast, follow that with a quick rub of garlic, and then top it with a mayo-free egg salad. The real secrets? Good eggs and proper cooking technique. Good eggs give you beautiful bright yellow yolks, and good technique helps you avoid the dreaded gray rings around them. If I want to take this sandwich on the go, I keep the components separate, with the egg salad chilled, until I'm ready to eat. If you are using extra-large eggs, let them cook for 10 minutes, instead of 7, before cooling and peeling.

Open-Face Egg Sandwich

WHOLE GRAIN TOAST, HERBS, YOGURT

2 tablespoons plain yogurt,
   plus more if needed

Fine-grain sea salt and freshly
   ground black pepper

2 tablespoons chopped fresh
   dill or chives, and/or a
   small pinch of fresh thyme,
   plus more if needed

4 extra-thin slices artisan
   whole grain bread

A bit of unsalted butter

1 clove garlic, peeled

4 large eggs, hard cooked and
   cooled (see box page 116)

Combine the yogurt, a couple pinches of salt, a small pinch of pepper, and (most of) whichever herb you choose in a small bowl. Set aside.

Toast the bread until it is deeply golden. Rub each piece with a bit of butter, then take the clove of garlic and rub it against each slice. Set aside.

Crack and peel each egg. Put them in a medium mixing bowl. Add the yogurt mixture and mash with a fork. Don't overdo it; you want the egg mixture to have some texture. If you need to add more yogurt to moisten the mixture, go for it, a small dollop at a time. Taste and add more salt, pepper, or herbs, if needed. Just before you're ready to eat, place one-quarter of the egg salad on each slice of bread and top with leftover herbs.

SERVES 2 TO 4

{ pictured on pages 58 and 59 }

I like to round out my pasta preparations with a good amount of vegetables and other fresh ingredients. Here, tortellini with ricotta-stuffed bellies are combined with blanched broccoli and asparagus, toasted nuts, avocado, and sprouts. The salad makes a great lunch and travels well.

Tortellini Salad

AVOCADO, SPROUTS, CILANTRO, PINE NUTS

Bring a large pot of water to a boil. Salt generously, add the tortellini, and cook according to the package instructions. About 30 seconds before the pasta is finished cooking, stir the asparagus and broccoli into the pot. Cook for the final 30 seconds, drain, and run under cold water just long enough to stop the cooking.

In the meantime, to make the dressing, use the flat side of your knife to mash the garlic along with a big pinch of salt into a paste. Whisk together the garlic paste, lemon juice, olive oil, and more salt, if needed. Set aside.

When you're ready to serve the salad, toss the pasta, asparagus, broccoli, and cilantro with about half of the dressing. Add more dressing to taste, if needed, and toss well. Add the sprouts, nuts, and avocado. Very gently toss a couple of times to distribute those ingredients throughout the salad and enjoy. Keep the extra dressing on hand to refresh leftovers; the pasta tends to absorb it overnight.

SERVES 4

Fine-grained sea salt

16 ounces / 455 g fresh ricotta-stuffed tortellini

8 to 10 asparagus spears, trimmed and cut into 1-inch / 2.5cm segments

1/2 head broccoli or equivalent broccolini, cut into small trees

1 small clove garlic

2 tablespoons fresh lemon juice

1/4 cup / 60 ml extra-virgin olive oil

Small handful of fresh cilantro or mint, chopped

Small handful of sprouts

1/3 cup / 1 ounce / 30 g pine nuts or almonds, toasted (see page 219)

1 medium ripe avocado, sliced into small pieces

I like to make this with spinach or whole wheat ricotta-stuffed tortellini, but the recipe is quite flexible. And while alfalfa sprouts are quite common, feel free to experiment with other types of sprouts.

I make this soup two ways: chunky and smooth. This is the chunky version, and I flavor it with red curry paste. For the smooth version, you can substitute green curry paste for the red, and puree the whole lot with an immersion blender before topping with the tofu croutons and serving. This chunky version is primarily a concession to aesthetics; when you puree the red curry with green-skinned vegetables, it makes for an off-colored soup. If you happen to have fresh basil on hand, sliver a small handful of it and use it as a finishing touch. A drizzle of basil oil is nice, too.

Summer Squash Soup

RED THAI CURRY, TOFU CROUTONS

8 ounces / 225 g extra-firm tofu, cut into ¹/₂-inch / 1cm cubes

Fine-grain sea salt

1 tablespoon red Thai curry paste, plus more if needed

3 tablespoons extra-virgin coconut oil or extra-virgin olive oil, plus more for the tofu croutons

3 large shallots, chopped

1¹/₂ pounds / 680 g (about 5 medium) yellow summer squash or zucchini, cut into ³/₄-inch / 2cm thick chunks

12 ounces / 340 g potatoes, unpeeled, cut into tiny cubes

4 cloves garlic, chopped

2 cups / 475 ml lightly flavored vegetable broth or water

1 (14-ounce / 415ml) can coconut milk

Season the tofu with a pinch of salt, toss with a small amount of oil, and cook in a large skillet over medium-high heat for about 5 minutes, until the pieces are browned on one side. Toss gently once or twice, and continue cooking until the tofu is firm, golden, and bouncy, 3 to 4 more minutes. Set aside.

Mash the curry paste into the coconut oil until the paste is well incorporated. Heat this paste in a large heavy soup pot over medium heat until fragrant, about 1 minute. Stir in the shallots and a couple of pinches of salt and sauté until the shallots are tender, another couple of minutes. Stir in the squash and potatoes and cook until the squash starts to get a tender, a few minutes. Stir in the garlic, then add the broth and coconut milk. Bring just to a boil, then lower the heat to a gentle simmer, stirring occasionally, until the potatoes are tender, about 15 minutes.

Taste and adjust the seasoning, adding more salt or curry paste, if needed. Serve each bowl topped with some of the tofu croutons.

SERVES 6

This is a simple wrap made with lavash, a thin, soft Middle Eastern flatbread, enveloping a chunky celery- and dill-accented chickpea salad. I keep my eyes open for whole wheat lavash; the thinner the better. Alternatively, you can substitute whole wheat tortillas or pita bread—pretty much anything flat, bendable, and edible that you can use to wrap or stuff with the chickpeas. On occasion, I'll toast the whole wrap (after stuffing) in a skillet with a bit of butter. You can make the filling a day or two ahead of time. It just keeps improving as the ingredients have a chance to intermingle.

Chickpea Wraps

WHOLE WHEAT LAVASH, CELERY, DILL, MUSTARD

3 cups / 15 oz / 425 g cooked chickpeas (see page 215), or 1½ (15-ounce / 425g) cans chickpeas, rinsed and drained

⅓ cup / 1.5 oz / 45 g chopped red onion or shallots

½ cup / 2 oz / 60 g chopped celery

2 tablespoons chopped fresh dill

1½ tablespoons Dijon-style mustard

⅔ cup / 5.5 ounces / 155 g plain yogurt

Scant ½ teaspoon fine-grain sea salt, plus more if needed

1 tablespoon fresh lemon juice, plus more if needed, and a bit of grated zest

4 pieces lavash flatbread, whole wheat tortillas, or whole wheat pitas

2 cups / 1 oz / 30 g mixed salad greens

Pulse two-thirds of the chickpeas in a food processor a few times, just enough to break them up. Transfer them to a large mixing bowl along with the remaining whole chickpeas. Stir in the onion, celery, and dill.

In a small bowl, whisk together the mustard, yogurt, and salt. Toss the chickpeas with about two-thirds of the yogurt mixture. Add the lemon juice and zest and toss again. Have a taste and add more salt or lemon juice, if needed.

Spread a bit of the remaining yogurt across each piece of lavash. Sprinkle each piece with one-quarter of the mixed greens (the yogurt will help hold the greens in place), top each of the four wraps with one-quarter of the chickpea mixture. Fold or roll into a wrap. If you are using pita bread, spread a bit of the yogurt dressing inside each pita half, tuck in the salad greens, and finish by filling with the chickpea salad.

SERVES 4

I enthusiastically adopted this as my go-to potato salad recipe not long after catching a glimpse of it in my friend Olivia's Flickr stream. Generous amounts of green beans, celery, cucumber, and tofu are tossed with a dill and caramelized-leek base. For you traditionalists, there is just enough mustard and red wine vinegar to give it that classic French potato salad flavor. I use the smallest pink potatoes I can find for a touch of added flare, but any small, waxy potatoes will work.

Mostly Not Potato Salad

DILL, LEEK, CELERY, MUSTARD, POTATOES, TOFU

4 small pink or red-skinned
  potatoes, unpeeled,
  quartered
Big handful of green beans,
  trimmed and sliced into
  1-inch / 2.5cm pieces
2 tablespoons whole grain
  mustard (see page 209)
2 tablespoons red wine
  vinegar
Extra-virgin olive oil
$^1/_2$ teaspoon natural cane
  sugar or agave nectar
Fine-grain sea salt
$^1/_4$ cup / .25 oz / 10 g finely
  chopped dill
1 small leek, white and tender
  green parts, trimmed and
  chopped
6 stalks celery, trimmed and
  diced
1 cucumber, unpeeled,
  seeded and cut into tiny
  cubes
6 ounces / 170 g baked or
  extra-firm tofu, cut into
  small cubes
1 tablespoon chopped fresh
  chives

Bring a pot of water to a rolling boil. Salt generously, add the potatoes, and cook until tender but not falling apart, about 10 minutes. Thirty seconds before the potatoes are done cooking, add the green beans to the pot. Drain the potatoes and beans and set aside.

In the meantime, make the dressing by whisking together the mustard, vinegar, 1 tablespoon olive oil, the sugar, and $^1/_4$ teaspoon salt in a bowl. Alternatively, combine the ingredients in a mason jar and shake until blended. Taste and adjust if needed.

In a large skillet, sauté the dill in a splash of olive oil over medium-high heat. Add a couple pinches of salt, stir in the leek, and sauté until golden and slightly crispy, 4 to 5 minutes.

In a large bowl, gently toss the potatoes and green beans, celery, cucumber, tofu, chives, and half of the leek with most of the dressing. Taste, and add a sprinkling of salt, if needed. Turn out onto a platter and finish with a final drizzle of dressing and the remaining leek. Serve chilled or at room temperature.

SERVES 4 TO 6

This is the salad to make when you stumble upon young, tender dandelion greens. Look for leaves that aren't much longer than a pencil, with waiflike stems. More mature dandelion greens can be a bit tough, and their backbones are more stalklike. If you can't find dandelion greens, there's no problem swapping in chopped chard, or spinach, or whatever greens happen to look best at your market; the selection will change throughout the year. Whatever you buy, be sure to give any unruly stems a quick trim. For something a bit more substantial, and to make this feisty salad a great one-dish meal, I like to top it with a crumbled hard-cooked egg.

Chickpeas & Dandelion Greens
RED PEPPER FLAKES & HOT OLIVE OIL DRESSING

Put the chickpeas in a medium bowl.

Take out a large skillet, and, while it is still cold, add the olive oil, garlic, red pepper flakes, and 2 big pinches of salt. Stir over medium heat until the garlic starts to sizzle; it should not begin to brown. Toss the dandelion greens into the skillet and stir until they begin to wilt, 15 seconds or so. Stir in the lemon zest.

Pour the greens over the chickpeas and toss. Taste, and add a bit more salt if needed. Transfer to a platter and seve warm or at room temperature.

SERVES 2 AS A MAIN DISH,
4 AS A SIDE DISH

2 cups / 10 oz / 280 g cooked chickpeas (see page 215), or 1 (15-ounce / 425g) can chickpeas, rinsed and drained

3 tablespoons extra-virgin olive oil

4 cloves garlic, finely chopped

1/2 teaspoon red pepper flakes

Fine-grain sea salt

3 or 4 handfuls of young dandelion leaves, stems trimmed

Grated zest of 1 lemon

One afternoon a local farmer said to me, "Cherries don't have a season. They have a moment." True enough. And when that moment reveals itself each year, you'll find me buying cherries by the flat. This salad features Bing cherries pureed into a bubble gum pink vinaigrette, then tossed with rice, spinach, toasted nuts, and torn cherries—with maybe a bit of crumbled goat cheese, too, if I'm in the mood. You can substitute just about any grain you like—brown rice, wild rice, red or black quinoa—but I lean toward dark-colored grains here. The cherry vinaigrette lends a funky pink cast to lighter-colored grains. The rice you see in the photo is sustainably farmed Black Japonica rice.

Whole Grain Rice Salad

SPINACH, BASIL, GOAT CHEESE, WALNUTS, CHERRY VINAIGRETTE

3½ cups / 17.5 oz / 500 g
   cooked whole grain rice
   (see page 218), heated
4 handfuls baby spinach,
   stems trimmed
⅔ cup / 3 oz / 85 g
   walnut halves, toasted
   (see page 219)
1½ cups / 7.5 oz / 210 g
   sweet cherries, pitted
½ cup / 120 ml extra-virgin
   olive oil
¼ cup / 60 ml white wine
   vinegar
Fine-grain sea salt
A few small basil leaves
A bit of goat cheese,
   crumbled (optional)

Combine the hot rice, spinach, and most of the walnuts in a large bowl. Toss until the spinach wilts a bit.

Make the cherry vinaigrette by combining one-third of the cherries, the olive oil, white wine vinegar, and ¼ teaspoon salt and blending until smooth. Add a generous splash of the dressing to the salad.

Tear the remaining cherries in half and stir most of them into the rice. Taste and add more salt, if needed. Turn the salad out onto a platter and finish with the last of the cherries, walnuts, basil, and goat cheese. Serve immediately.

SERVES 6

You can buy cooked wild and brown rice in the freezer or dry goods sections of many stores now. For a salad like this, I prefer to cook the rice from scratch, but using a good-quality store-bought cooked rice can still be delicious. Instructions for cooking wild rice and brown rice from scratch are on page 218.

My friend Malinda showed me how to make this salad one rainy weekend while sharing a rustic cabin with a handful of friends, two dogs, one baby, and quite a bit of good wine. My enthusiasm for it can't be overstated. For such a short ingredient list, there's an impressive range of textures and flavors. There's the peppery kick of the arugula playing off the lemon, olive oil, and cool dill. Then there are the bright anise notes from the fennel, the crunch of the pine nuts, and the creamy tanginess of the feta.

To make quick work of the slicing required here, I sometimes use my mandoline. You can certainly use a knife, but do your best to slice very, very thinly—not quite "see-through" thin, but close.

Shaved Fennel Salad

ZUCCHINI COINS, FETA, PINE NUTS

1 medium-large zucchini, sliced into paper-thin coins

2 small fennel bulbs, trimmed and shaved paper-thin

$2/3$ cup / .5 oz / 15 g loosely packed chopped fresh dill

$1/3$ cup / 80 ml fresh lemon juice (about 3 juicy lemons), plus more if needed

$1/3$ cup / 80 ml extra-virgin olive oil, plus more if needed

Fine-grain sea salt

4 or 5 generous handfuls arugula

Honey, if needed

$1/2$ cup / 2 oz / 60 g pine nuts, toasted (see page 219)

$1/3$ cup / 2 oz / 60 g feta cheese, crumbled

Combine the zucchini, fennel, and dill in a bowl and toss with the lemon juice, olive oil, and $1/4$ teaspoon salt. Set aside and let marinate for 20 minutes, or up to an hour.

When you are ready to serve the salad, put the arugula in a large salad bowl. Scoop all of the zucchini and fennel onto the arugula, and pour most of the lemon juice dressing on top of that. Toss gently but thoroughly. Taste and adjust with more of the dressing, olive oil, lemon juice, or salt, if needed. If your lemons are particularly tart (which happens to me on occasion), you may need to counter the pucker-factor by adding a tiny drizzle of honey into the salad at this point. Let your taste buds guide you. Serve topped with the pine nuts and feta.

SERVES 4 TO 6

Here I combine big chunks of fragrant melon with feta, kalamata olives, and a bit of chopped mint. It's the sort of thing to make at the peak of summer when a wide range of melons is available—honeydew, cantaloupe, and ambrosias. Simple, with clean, clear flavors, it's perfect served with a nice Riesling or any crisp and bubbly white wine.

Look for brick-shaped feta, which is easy to cut into small and somewhat defined cubes.

Mixed Melon Bowl

MINT, LEMON JUICE, FETA, KALAMATA OLIVES

Put the melon in a large serving bowl and toss gently with the mint and lemon juice. If you're serving the salad family-style, sprinkle the feta and olives across the top of the melon. Alternatively, plate the melon individually, insuring each serving has a few pieces of feta as well as a few olives. You want to get all of the flavors in each bite.

SERVES 4

2½ pounds / 1.25 kg melon (mixed varietals), peeled, seeded, cut into 1-inch / 2.5cm chunks, and chilled

8 fresh mint leaves, finely chopped (about 1 tablespoon)

1 teaspoon fresh lemon juice

1½ ounces / 45 g feta cheese, cut into ½-inch / 1cm cubes

12 kalamata olives, pitted and torn in half

Pass on watermelons for this particular preparation; it's a bad neighbor, prone to staining nearby melon pieces. Also, as far as texture is concerned, creamy-textured melons are preferred alongside the feta. But, if you're a true watermelon lover, take the salad in that direction entirely. Forget the mixed approach, and use 100 percent watermelon instead.

This pasta salad is right at home at just about any potluck or party—and it's particularly happy parked next to a bowl brimming with a leafy green salad. I made it first for my sister's baby shower, and a dozen times since. As far as choosing the right type of ravioli, I keep red pepper ravioli with chard filling on hand (in the freezer) just for this salad. I like the play between the red pepper and the zesty lemon-cilantro pesto. But you can take the idea in a number of directions, and both spinach and whole wheat ravioli are worthy substitutes. If you can imagine the filling going well with the cilantro pesto, you're probably in safe territory.

Ravioli Salad

BLACK OLIVES & PEPITAS

Bring a large pot of water to boil. In the meantime, make the cilantro pesto. Combine most of the pepitas, cilantro, Parmesan cheese, garlic, lemon juice, and a splash of the olive oil and blend with an immersion blender (or in a food processor or standard blender) until smooth. Continue blending as you gradually drizzle in the remaining olive oil, until the pesto comes together into a vibrant green sauce. Taste and add salt or more lemon juice, if needed.

When the water boils, salt it generously, add the ravioli, and boil until they float and are cooked through, usually just 1 or 2 minutes. Drain immediately and while still hot, toss with a big spoonful of the pesto. Allow the pesto to soak in a bit. Then add another 1/2 cup / 120 ml of the pesto along with most of the black olives. Toss well, but gently, and then decide whether you want to add more pesto or not.

Turn everything out into a large bowl or platter and sprinkle with the remaining olives, pepitas, and flowers. Serve warm or at room temperature. Reserve the remaining pesto for tossing with leftovers.

SERVES 4 TO 6

1/3 cup / 1.5 oz / 45 g pepitas, toasted (see page 219)

1 cup / .5 oz / 15 g lightly packed cilantro leaves and stems

1/3 cup / .5 oz / 15 g freshly grated Parmesan cheese

3 cloves garlic, peeled

2 tablespoons fresh lemon juice, plus more if needed

2/3 cup / 160 ml extra-virgin olive oil

Fine-grain sea salt

16 ounces / 450 g fresh or frozen ravioli

1/2 cup / 3 oz / 85 g oil-cured black olives, pitted and torn or chopped

Thyme or chive flowers, to garnish (optional)

This is the sort of dish you can see from across the room.
Festive and colorful, the bright yellow spilt peas in the salad act as a beacon.
To keep things lively, I use a version of cilantro pesto here that is slightly
spicier than the one in my Ravioli Salad (page 75).
If you don't have the time or inclination to cook the split yellow peas
from scratch, canned white beans (or even chickpeas) can
take their place with good results.

Yellow Split Peas & Greens

MIXED GREENS, SERRANO CHILE, LEMON JUICE

1¹/₂ cups / 10.5 oz / 300 g
  dried split yellow peas,
  rinsed and picked over
Fine-grain sea salt
1 cup / 4.5 oz / 125 g pepitas,
  toasted (see page 219)
1 cup / .5 oz / 15 g lightly
  packed cilantro leaves and
  stems
¹/₃ cup / .5 oz / 15 g freshly
  grated Parmesan cheese
3 cloves garlic, peeled
1 tablespoon fresh lemon
  juice
1 small serrano chile, mostly
  seeded and deveined
²/₃ cup / 160 ml extra-virgin
  olive oil
2 large handfuls mixed salad
  greens

Bring 5 cups / 1.25 liters water to a boil in a large
saucepan. Add the yellow split peas and simmer,
uncovered, for 20 to 30 minutes, until tender. Drain
and salt to taste. Make the cilantro pesto by combining
one-third of the toasted pepitas, the cilantro, Parmesan
cheese, garlic, lemon juice, ¹/₄ teaspoon salt, a splash of
the olive oil, and the chile and blend with an immersion
blender (or in a food processor or standard blender) until
smooth. Continue blending as you gradually drizzle
in the olive oil, until the pesto comes together into a
vibrant green sauce. Taste and add a pinch or two of salt,
if needed.

In a large bowl, toss the yellow split peas and
remaining pepitas with two-thirds of the pesto. Keep
tossing until everything is coated. Add the salad greens
and gently toss again. Taste and add more pesto, if
needed. You'll have a bit of extra pesto, which can be
used to refresh any leftovers.

SERVES 4 TO 6

{ pictured on pages 76 and 77 }

A few hours north of San Francisco, on the California coast near Anchor Bay (not far from some of the places you see photographed in this book), I had a sandwich on a modest café patio. The sandwich was a quirky mix of oven-roasted tomatoes, peanut butter dressing, grilled tofu, and sprouts, all pinned between two slices of multigrain bread. It was odd but completely delicious. I liked it enough to rework it into this twist on panzanella, the much-loved Italian bread salad.

Panzanella

GRILLED TOFU, SUNFLOWER SPROUTS, PEANUT BUTTER, OVEN-ROASTED TOMATOES

Brush the bread slices on both sides with the olive oil, sprinkle with salt, and toast on a medium-hot grill until each side is golden, crunchy, and has grill marks. Tear the bread into bite-size chunks and set aside.

Brush the tofu with olive oil and place on the grill. Cook until the tofu is golden on the bottom with nice grill marks, about 7 minutes (rotate the tofu 90 degrees halfway through the grilling of each side to get crisscross marks). Flip, cook the other sides, brush the sides facing up with more olive oil, and cook until the bottom is golden as well, another 5 minutes or so. Remove from the grill, cut into 1/2-inch / 1cm pieces, and place in a large bowl.

Make the peanut dressing by combining the peanut butter, vinegar, garlic, sesame oil, red pepper flakes, and 1/4 teaspoon salt in a medium bowl. Thin with the hot water; the amount you'll need depends on the consistency of your peanut butter. I like the dressing to be the consistency of melted ice cream. Taste and make any adjustments if needed—more salt, more red pepper flakes, and so on.

Just before serving, pour a generous amount of the dressing over the tofu, and toss it gently, but well. It should look quite overdressed at this point. Add the bread and gently toss again. Turn out onto a platter and top with the sprouts and then the tomatoes. Serve at room temperature.

SERVES 4 TO 6

Two thick slices artisan multigrain or whole wheat bread (about 6 oz / 170 g total)

2 tablespoons extra-virgin olive oil, plus more for the tofu

Fine-grain sea salt

12-ounce / 340 g block extra-firm tofu, sliced into 4 slabs

1/3 cup / 2.5 oz / 70 g creamy peanut butter

2 tablespoons brown rice vinegar

1 clove garlic, chopped

1/4 teaspoon toasted sesame oil

1/4 teaspoon red pepper flakes, plus more if needed

1/3 to 1/2 cup / 80 to 120 ml hot water

1 1/2 lightly packed cups / 3 oz / 85 g sunflower sprouts or other sprouts

1/2 cup / 3 oz / 85 g oven-roasted tomatoes (see page 231)

I take minimal credit for this unlikely combination of ingredients. One afternoon I asked a farmer at my neighborhood market what he liked to do with the purple peacock kale he was selling. He convincingly rattled off something close to this, and I now find myself making it regularly. Here's what I've learned. You can use whatever type of kale you like. I love the purple peacock, but the more common lacinato kale gives off a subtle banana scent that goes particularly well with the toasted coconut. To make a more substantial meal of the salad, stir the finished baked kale into a couple cups of cooked farro, wild rice, or quinoa—whatever you have on hand, really. It's also great alongside a bit of grilled tofu or over a bowl of soba noodles. IMPORTANT: If you can only find finely shredded unsweetened coconut (it's more common), reduce the amount to 1/2 cup / 1.5 oz / 45 g.

Kale Salad

TOASTED COCONUT & SESAME OIL

1/3 cup / 80 ml extra-virgin olive oil

1 teaspoon toasted sesame oil

2 tablespoons shoyu, tamari, or soy sauce

3 1/2 lightly packed cups / 3.5 oz / 100 g chopped kale, stems trimmed, large ribs removed

1 1/2 cups / 3 oz / 85 g unsweetened large-flake coconut

2 cups / 9 oz / 255 g cooked farro or other whole grain (optional)

Preheat the oven to 350°F / 180°C with two racks in the top third of the oven.

In a small bowl or jar, whisk or shake together the olive oil, sesame oil, and shoyu. Put the kale and coconut in a large bowl and toss well with about two-thirds of the olive oil mixture.

Spread the kale evenly across two baking sheets. Bake for 12 to 18 minutes, until the coconut is deeply golden brown, tossing once or twice along the way. If the kale mixture on the top baking sheet begins to get too browned, move it to the lower rack.

Remove from the oven and transfer the kale mixture to a medium bowl. Taste. If you feel it needs a bit more dressing, add some and toss. Place the farro on a serving platter and top with the tossed kale. Serve warm.

SERVES 4

Make this simple salad when strawberries are at their peak of sweetness, although keep in mind that strawberries can be deceptive. Some of the most stunning, ruby-red berries I've tasted have been quite tart. Sample a berry or two before buying. And when strawberry season is over, it's worth keeping your eyes open for dried strawberries. A generous handful, chopped, works nicely in place of the fresh berries. You can run a vegetable peeler along the length of a wedge of Parmesan to make nice curls of cheese, or, if you live somewhere where you can get good local goat cheese, replace the Parmesan with crumbled, soft goat cheese. Its tangy, chalky creaminess goes perfectly alongside the berries and balsamic vinegar.

Mixed Green Salad

STRAWBERRIES, PARMESAN, BLACK PEPPER, BALSAMIC VINEGAR

1 shallot, finely chopped

1/4 teaspoon freshly ground black pepper

Scant 1/2 teaspoon fine-grain sea salt

3 tablespoons balsamic vinegar, preferably aged

3 tablespoons extra-virgin olive oil

5 handfuls / 2.5 oz / 70 g mixed salad greens

1/3 cup / 1 oz / 30 g sliced or slivered almonds, toasted (see page 219)

12 small to medium perfect strawberries, hulled and sliced pencil-thick

1/3 cup / .5 oz / 15 g shaved Parmesan cheese curls

Whisk together the shallot, pepper, salt, and balsamic vinegar in a small bowl and set aside for 5 to 10 minutes. Whisk in the oil, a bit at a time, until the dressing comes together.

Just before serving, combine most of the dressing with the salad greens in a large salad bowl. Toss gently but thoroughly; you want to be sure all the lettuce is coated. Add the almonds, strawberries, and Parmesan and gently toss once or twice more, just enough to coat a bit and distribute equally throughout the bowl.

SERVES 4

This late-summer bowl of creamy-fleshed black beans, crumbled feta cheese, tangy-sweet oven-roasted cherry tomatoes, crunchy seeds, and lemon zest is perfect for picnics. It's also worth noting that you can prepare all of the components a day or two ahead of time. If you don't have the time or inclination to oven-roast the tomatoes, you can use oil-packed sun-dried tomatoes. Use about 1/2 cup / 2 oz / 60 g along with 2 tablespoons of the olive oil, and chop them into pieces not much larger than a pencil eraser.

Because there aren't more than a handful of ingredients here, it's best to cook the black beans from scratch. You can certainly substitute canned beans, and the results will still be delicious, but if at all possible, source some good dried beans and take it from there. For a real treat, you might also substitute freshly cooked shell beans when those are in season.

Black Bean Salad

OVEN-ROASTED TOMATOES, ALMONDS, LEMON ZEST, FETA

In a large bowl, toss the beans with most of the tomatoes (and their olive oil), pepitas, 1/4 teaspoon salt, the lemon zest, and lemon juice. Taste. If you think the salad needs a bit more salt, lemon juice, or extra-virgin olive oil, go ahead and add some, a little at a time. Finish the beans by sprinkling them with the remaining tomatoes and feta. Serve at room temperature.

SERVES 4 TO 6

4 cups / 22 oz / 625 g cooked black beans (see page 215), or 2 (15-ounce / 425g) cans, rinsed and drained

3/4 cup / 4.5 oz / 125 g Oven-Roasted Cherry Tomatoes (page 231), with olive-oil sludge

3/4 cup / 3.5 oz / 100 g pepitas and/or almonds, toasted (see page 219)

Fine-grain sea salt

Grated zest of 1 small lemon

1 tablespoon fresh lemon juice, plus more if needed

Extra-virgin olive oil, if needed

1/3 cup / 1.5 oz / 45 g crumbled feta cheese

This is the sort of simple dish I find myself enjoying on the most blustery of San Francisco afternoons. I use whatever type of beans I have on hand. Creamy, thin-skinned Mayacobas or flageolets are my favorites for this particular preparation, but well-drained canned cannellini beans or chickpeas are reasonable substitutes as well. If you're in the mood for a stew, stir any leftovers into a cup or two of good-flavored vegetable broth.

White Beans & Cabbage

PARMESAN, POTATOES, SHALLOTS

2 tablespoons extra-virgin olive oil, clarified butter (see page 224), or unsalted butter

4 ounces / 115 g potatoes, unpeeled, scrubbed, and cut into tiny cubes

Fine-grain sea salt

1 large shallot, thinly sliced

2 cups / 12 oz / 340 g cooked and cooled white beans (see page 215), or 1 (15-ounce / 425g) can white beans, rinsed and drained

3 cups / 8 oz / 225 g very finely shredded green cabbage

A bit of freshly grated Parmesan cheese

Pour the olive oil into a large skillet over medium-high heat. Add the potatoes and a big pinch of salt. Toss, cover, and cook until the potatoes are cooked through, 5 to 8 minutes. Be sure to scrape the pan and toss the potatoes once or twice along the way so all sides get color. Stir in the shallot and the beans. Let the beans cook in a single layer for a couple minutes, until they brown a bit, then scrape and toss again. Cook until the beans are nicely browned and a bit crispy on all sides. Stir in the cabbage and cook for another minute, or until the cabbage loses a bit of its structure. Serve dusted with Parmesan.

SERVES 4

This is one of the most appetizing ways to get roasted potatoes, broccoli, and eggs onto the same plate. Think French-dressed egg salad meets potato salad, punctuated by plenty of broccoli. Feel free to swap in asparagus or leeks for the broccoli when in season, and use the tiniest fingerling potatoes you can get your hands on. If you can't find the variety of fresh herbs called for, just use an equivalent amount of the ones you can find.

Broccoli Gribiche

ROASTED POTATOES, RED WINE VINEGAR, CAPERS, MUSTARD

1¹/₂ pounds / 680 g small
    fingerling potatoes,
    unpeeled, scrubbed
    and dried

¹/₂ cup / 120 ml plus
    2 tablespoons extra-virgin
    olive oil

Fine-grain sea salt

12 ounces / 340 g broccoli
    florets

4 large eggs, hard cooked and
    peeled (see box page 116)

2 tablespoons red wine
    vinegar

1 teaspoon Dijon-style
    mustard

1 tablespoon capers, chopped

2 shallots, chopped

1 tablespoon chopped fresh
    parsley

1 tablespoon chopped fresh
    tarragon

1 tablespoon chopped fresh
    chervil or chives

Preheat the oven to 400°F / 205°C degrees with two racks in the top and middle of the oven.

If the potatoes aren't tiny, slice them into pieces no larger than your thumb. Use your hands to toss the potatoes with 1 tablespoon of the olive oil, sprinkle with a big pinch of salt, and turn out onto a baking sheet. Roast until they are cooked through and starting to brown, about 30 minutes. About 15 minutes before you think the potatoes are done, toss the broccoli with 1 tablespoon of the olive oil, sprinkle with salt, arrange in a single layer on a baking sheet and place in the oven as well. You are aiming to have the potatoes and broccoli finish cooking at (roughly) the same time. I like the broccoli a touch charred.

To make the dressing, mash just the yolk of one of the hard-cooked eggs in a medium bowl. Very, very slowly add the remaining ¹/₂ cup / 120 ml olive oil, beating constantly; the dressing should look smooth and glossy. Whisk in the vinegar, then the mustard. Stir in the capers, shallots, herbs, and ¹/₄ teaspoon salt.

Coarsely chop the remaining eggs and egg white, and fold them into the dressing. Put the warm potatoes and broccoli in a large bowl and gently toss with three-quarters of the dressing. Taste, adjust the flavors, and add more dressing, if needed. Serve turned out onto a platter or in a bowl.

SERVES 6

I should mention there are as many ways to approach a traditional French gribiche sauce as there are French cooks. Some simply chop all the ingredients and mix them together and that's completely fine. I like to make a creamy emulsion with one of the egg yolks and go from there.

There aren't more than a handful of ingredients at play here, but they come together to create my favorite tacos. Steve Sando, the guy to thank for all the Rancho Gordo ingredients I love, taught me to make them. In his tacos, he used beautiful chanterelle mushrooms. But I can now say they're still pretty darn great with just about any sliced mushrooms: mixed wild mushrooms, porcini, or even plain little brown ones. I'm a fan of a good amount of chile heat, but if you're sensitive to spicy foods, scale back and use less than 1 chile. Steve says it best, "Serranos are technically hotter than jalapeños, but they have a much more lovely heat that attacks your whole being, not just your mouth. I like jalapeños, too, but they're a little like being kicked in the mouth by an irritated donkey. I always tell people who think they don't like heat to start with the serranos, even though they're supposed to be hotter."

Make the effort to find Mexican oregano—it's worth it. And, if you can find real Cotija cheese, use it in place of the Parmesan. But look for cheese from the actual town of Cotija. The domestic brands aren't nearly as good.

The mushrooms are also great in crepes (see page 50), over quinoa, in risotto, or over pasta.

{ pictured on pages 90 and 91 }

Chanterelle Tacos

SERRANO CHILE, GARLIC, PARMESAN

Heat the olive oil and butter in a large skillet over medium-high heat. When hot, add the onion, chile, garlic, and ¼ teaspoon salt. Sauté until the onions are translucent, a few minutes. Increase the heat to high, add the mushrooms, stir well, and cook until the mushrooms release their liquid, and then brown, about 5 minutes more. Stir a few times along the way, but don't overdo it; you want the mushrooms to be deeply browned. Remove from the heat, then rub the Mexican oregano between your palms and let it cascade down into the mushroom mixture. Taste and add a bit more salt, if needed.

Spoon the mixture into the warmed tortillas and sprinkle the Parmesan over all of the tacos.

SERVES 4

2 tablespoons extra-virgin olive oil

2 tablespoons unsalted butter

½ white onion, finely chopped

1 small serrano chile, finely chopped

2 cloves garlic, finely chopped

Fine-grain sea salt

12 ounces / 340 g chanterelles or mixed wild mushrooms, sliced

1½ teaspoons dried Mexican oregano

8 corn tortillas, warmed

½ cup / 1 oz / 30 g freshly grated Parmesan cheese

TO WARM TORTILLAS, wrap the stack of tortillas in a barely damp kitchen towel. Place in a heavy pot over very low heat, cover, and let warm for a few minutes, or until you are ready to use them.

This is a stand-up way to put a couple heads of broccoli to use. I make a broccoli-based pesto, then mix it, along with the leftover florets, into a bowl of orzo pasta. Beyond that, it's quite straightforward—a bit of avocado brings an element of creaminess and the pine nuts add a bit of crunch. If you can't find orzo, substitute another tiny pasta, or even farro or wheat berries.

You can cook the pasta, blanch the broccoli, and make the pesto ahead of time, if needed. And, if you're looking for something more substantial, top with a poached egg or two (see pages 222 and 223).

Orzo Salad

WHOLE WHEAT ORZO, BROCCOLI PESTO, LEMON, AVOCADO, CRÈME FRAÎCHE

Bring a large pot of water to boil. Salt generously, add the orzo, and cook according to the package instructions. Drain, rinse with cold water, and drain well again.

In the meantime, cook the broccoli. Bring ³/4 cup / 180 ml water to a boil in a large pot. Add a big pinch of salt and stir in the broccoli. Cover and cook for 1 minute, just long enough to take off the raw edge. Quickly drain the broccoli in a strainer and run under cold water to stop the cooking. Drain well and set aside.

To make the pesto, combine 2 cups / 7 oz / 200 g of the cooked broccoli, the garlic, most of the pine nuts, the Parmesan, ¹/4 teaspoon salt, and 2 tablespoons of the lemon juice in a food processor. Drizzle in the olive oil and crème fraîche and pulse until smooth.

Just before serving, toss the orzo and remaining cooked broccoli florets with about two-thirds of the broccoli pesto and the lemon zest. Thin with a bit of warm water if you like, then taste and adjust if needed. You might want to add a bit more salt, or an added drizzle of lemon juice, or more pesto. Gently fold in the avocado. Turn out into a bowl or onto a platter and top with the remaining pine nuts.

Fine-grained sea salt

1¹/2 cups / 9 oz / 255 g whole wheat orzo

5 cups / 11 oz / 310 g raw broccoli cut into small florets and stems

2 cloves garlic, peeled

²/3 cup / 3.5 oz / 100 g pine nuts, toasted (see page 219)

¹/3 cup / .5 oz / 15 g freshly grated Parmesan cheese

Juice of 1 lemon

¹/4 cup / 60 ml extra-virgin olive oil

¹/4 cup / 2 oz / 60 g crème fraîche (see page 226)

Grated zest of 1 lemon

1 small ripe avocado, peeled, pitted, and sliced

SERVES 6

I'm always looking for something to slather my favorite dill butter on, and this rye soda bread is just the thing. Soda breads are relatively quick to make; the dough comes together in a fraction of the time it takes to preheat your oven. No two loaves are quite the same, and they're meant to be imperfect—with a few cracks and crags here and there. If you've ever thought you don't have time to bake bread, I suggest starting here. I make a couple loaves a week, pretty much whenever the fancy strikes.

I like lots of good, crunchy crust, so I slash the dough a few times just before placing the bread in the hot oven. As it rises and spreads, the bread develops nearly twice as much crust as it does without the extra cuts. A loaf usually lasts a couple days, and any leftover makes great bread crumbs (see page 219) or strata (see page 33).

Rye Soda Bread

RYE FLOUR & BUTTERMILK

2$^{1}/_{3}$ cups / 9.75 oz / 275 g rye flour

1$^{3}/_{4}$ cups / 8 oz / 225 g unbleached all-purpose flour, plus more for dusting and kneading

1$^{3}/_{4}$ teaspoons baking soda

1$^{1}/_{4}$ teaspoons fine-grain sea salt

2 cups / 475 ml buttermilk, plus more for brushing

Preheat the oven to 400°F / 205°C with a rack in the middle of the oven.

Sift the flours, baking soda, and salt into a large bowl. Make a well in the flour and pour in the buttermilk. Stir just until everything comes together into a dough. Turn out onto a lightly floured countertop and knead for 30 seconds or so, just long enough for the dough to come together into a cohesive, slightly flattened ball without many cracks or fissures.

Lightly flour a baking sheet and place the ball of dough on the flour. Brush all over the top and sides with buttermilk and sprinkle generously with flour, 2 tablespoons or so. Slice four deep slashes across the top of the dough, two-thirds of the way through the loaf, as if you were slicing a pie into eight wedges; just be careful not to slice all the way through.

Bake for about 30 minutes, then quickly (without letting all the hot air out of the oven), move the rack and the bread up a level, so the top of the bread gets nice and toasted. Bake for another 20 minutes, or until a hard crust forms and the bread is baked through. It will feel very solid and sound hollow when you knock on its base. Cool on a wire rack and enjoy with a good slathering of dill butter (recipe follows).

MAKES 1 LOAF

Dill Butter

DILL, BUTTER, FARMER CHEESE, CHIVES, SHALLOTS

In a small bowl, mash together the dill, chives, shallots, butter, and salt. Mix until the herbs are evenly distributed throughout the butter. Crumble the cheese on top of the butter and stir a few times, just long enough to work the cheese into the butter, but keep the cheese a bit chunky. The dill butter will keep, refrigerated, for up to a week, but bring it back to room temperature before using.

MAKES ABOUT ¾ CUP / 6 OZ / 170 G

1½ tablespoons finely chopped fresh dill

1½ tablespoons finely chopped fresh chives

1½ tablespoons finely chopped shallots

½ cup / 4 oz / 115 g unsalted butter, at room temperature

¼ teaspoon fine-grain sea salt

⅓ cup / 2 oz / 60 g semisoft farmer cheese or mild, soft goat cheese

SNACKS

snacks

WHEN IT COMES TO FOOD, my day typically looks like this: breakfast, snack, lunch, snack, snack, dinner. I do my best to eat something substantial every 2 to 3 hours. And I've found if I don't let huge amounts of time pass without eating, I'm not overly hungry when I sit down for a proper meal.

When I snack poorly, the rest of my eating habits are quick to follow. And, just know, I'm by no means immune to the occasional sugar-bender. Pie for breakfast? It can happen to the best of us. But if I snack smartly throughout the day, I don't crave sugar and sweets quite as much.

Some of the snacks I reach for aren't very exciting: for example, a heaping spoon of nut butter. I like my snacks to have a good amount of fat and some protein, and nut butters do the job. When I snack on crackers and chips I'm often hungry 10 minutes later, so if there's a super-starchy component to my snack, I balance it out with some beans or lentils, or eggs, or avocado.

I do my best to cover 4 to 5 miles (8 km) on foot a day most days. Sometimes that means a long walk taking photos, or bundling my nephew into his stroller and pushing him the two miles to a favorite coffee shop. On other days, I cover the that same distance in an hour—I put on my sneakers, jog, shower, and I'm done. At first read, all this might not seem directly related to snacking, but it is. I'm reliant on good snacks before and after exercise to keep me going.

I've included a range of snacks in this chapter. Some are good for between-meal sustenance, and a good number are also party, picnic, and potluck appropriate.

This recipe is loosely inspired by a spicy curried avocado preparation I came across in Julie Sahni's *Classic Indian Vegetarian and Grain Cooking*. Its success really depends on buying ripe avocados. When your avocados are perfectly creamy in texture, they end up melding with the green chiles, garlic, onions, and mustard seeds beautifully.

Avocados and Mustard Seeds

SERRANO CHILE, CURRY POWDER, LEMON JUICE

2 ripe avocados

2 teaspoons fresh lemon juice

Scant 1/2 teaspoon fine-grain
    sea salt

1/2 cup / .25 oz / 10 g coarsely
    chopped fresh cilantro

1 tablespoon clarified butter
    (see page 224) or extra-
    virgin coconut oil

1 teaspoon black or brown
    mustard seeds

1 small yellow onion, minced

2 cloves garlic, finely
    chopped

1 teaspoon Indian curry
    powder

1 small serrano chile, minced

Cut each avocado in half, remove the pit, and scoop the flesh into a small bowl. Add the lemon juice, salt, and most of the cilantro. Mash the avocados a bit with a fork, but don't overdo it—you want the mixture to be quite chunky. Set aside.

Heat the clarified butter in a skillet over medium-high heat. When it is hot, add the mustard seeds. Keep a lid on hand because the seeds will scatter as they pop. When the spattering stops, after about a minute, stir in the onion and sauté for 2 to 3 minutes, until the onion is translucent. Stir in the garlic, curry powder, and chile. Count to ten, and then remove from heat. Stir in the avocado mixture, but just barely, and transfer to a serving bowl. Serve warm or at room temperature.

MAKES ABOUT 2 CUPS / 14 OZ / 400 G

I typically enjoy this as a snack alongside a bit of toasted naan, lavash, or Pita Chips (page 108), but I'd be holding out on you if I didn't say a spoonful is perfect in a bowl of brown rice or spread on a hot corn tortilla.

I put my mortar and pestle to work quite often making batches of the fragrant, nut-centric Egyptian spice blend called *dukkah*. Some days I add it to cottage cheese along with a couple torn olives. Other days, I use it as a dipping spice with bread and extra-virgin olive oil. I've also come to enjoy it sprinkled generously across hard-cooked eggs that have been sliced in half and drizzled with a bit of olive oil or hazelnut oil. Give it a try. This recipe makes enough *dukkah* for 2 dozen eggs, so, if I may sneak in a little side note here, save some *dukkah* in a vintage jar for giving as a nice hostess or housewarming gift.

Hard-Cooked Eggs with Dukkah

HAZELNUTS, MINT, MIXED SEEDS

$^1/_4$ cup / 1 oz / 30 g hazelnuts

2 tablespoons coriander
   seeds

2 tablespoons white sesame
   seeds

1 tablespoon cumin seeds

$^1/_2$ teaspoon fennel seeds

Scant $1^1/_2$ teaspoons black
   peppercorns

$^1/_2$ teaspoon dried mint

$^1/_2$ teaspoon fine-grain sea
   salt, plus more if needed

6 large eggs, hard cooked
   (see box page 116)

Extra-virgin olive oil or
   hazelnut oil, to drizzle

Flaky sea salt, to finish
   (optional)

Heat a large, heavy skillet over medium heat. Add the hazelnuts and toast until slightly browned and fragrant. Transfer to a small bowl and let cool completely. Repeat with the coriander seeds, sesame seeds, cumin seeds, fennel seeds, and the peppercorns, toasting each separately and allowing each to cool completely. Put the peppercorns in a mortar and pound until crushed. Add the nuts and seeds, along with the mint and salt, and crush some more to a coarse consistency. Alternatively, you can pulse in a food processor, but don't allow the mixture to become a paste.

Peel the eggs carefully, cut each one in half, and set cut-side up on a serving plate.

To serve, sprinkle the eggs generously with *dukkah*, drizzle with olive oil, and sprinkle with the tiniest bit of flaky sea salt if you happen to have some. Season with a bit more salt if you think the eggs could use it after the first bite.

Dukkah will keep in an airtight container in a cool place for up to 1 month.

MAKES 12 SERVINGS

I make these chips frequently. Slice and toss onto the baking pan—work quickly and you can have a batch in the oven in 2 minutes. The secret here is coating bite-size pieces of pita bread with a garlic-spiked blend of olive oil and melted butter. The butter gives the chips a richness that you can't get otherwise. This straightforward version is flavored with just salt and garlic, but you can take the basic idea in many directions. Season the pitas with spices, use an infused oil, or cut the pitas into whatever shape you like— wedges or strips, thick or thin. They are great in place of croutons, and perfect alongside just about any dip.
Make pita chips no more than a few hours before serving. They lose a bit of their crunch after spending any amount of time in a plastic bag.

Pita Chips

GARLIC, OLIVE OIL, BUTTER, SEA SALT

3 (7-inch / 18cm) whole wheat pitas, cut into bite-size strips or wedges

2 tablespoons unsalted butter, melted

3 tablespoons extra-virgin olive oil

1 clove garlic, finely chopped

Very scant 1/2 teaspoon fine-grain sea salt

Preheat the oven to 350°F / 180°C degrees with a rack in bottom third of the oven.

Put the pita pieces in a large bowl. Whisk together the butter, olive oil, garlic, and salt. Pour the mixture over the pita pieces and gently toss for 20 to 30 seconds, until well coated. Turn the pita pieces out onto a large baking sheet and arrange in a single layer.

Bake for 10 to 15 minutes, until the chips are deeply golden, tossing once along the way. Remove from oven and let cool.

SERVES 4

These are the least perfect chips you'll ever make. They never quite crisp up entirely, have a tendency to go from barely baked to burned in a blink, and they shrink in size, leaving you with half the chips you thought you'd get out of the batch. But their roasted buttery sweetness make them too good not to include here. Spritzed with lime and sprinkled with a bit of smoked paprika, they're even better.

Turnip Chips

SMOKED PAPRIKA & LIME JUICE

Preheat the oven to 425°F / 220°C with two racks set in the middle of the oven.

Using a mandoline or by hand, slice the turnips into uniform slices, none any thicker than two credit cards stacked on top of one another. If you are slicing by hand, cut the turnip in half and rest each half cut side down so they don't roll around; this makes for easier slicing. Toss the slices in a large bowl with the olive oil and salt and arrange in a single layer on two baking sheets.

Bake for 12 minutes, check, and then continue to bake until the chips are deeply golden. It usually takes somewhere between 5 and 15 minutes more, depending on the thickness of the slices.

Remove from the oven, sprinkle with a light dusting of paprika and a small spritz of lime juice, and toss gently. The chips crisp up a bit as they cool, but I like them best warm.

SERVES 2

4 medium turnips (about
    1½ pounds / 680 g), well
    scrubbed
3 tablespoons olive oil
    or clarified butter
    (see page 224)
¼ teaspoon fine-grain sea
    salt
A couple pinches of smoked
    paprika (pimenton)
Squeeze of lime

This is a simple pureed white bean dip made special by inviting rosemary and garlic-infused olive oil to play along. It's fragrant, easy to make, and a good companion for Pita Chips (page 108). The beans can be cooked from scratch, or you can use canned beans.

White Bean Spread
ROSEMARY & TOASTED ALMONDS

¹/₄ cup / 60 ml extra-virgin olive oil

1 teaspoon chopped fresh rosemary

1 clove garlic, finely chopped

2 cups / 12 oz / 340 g cooked white beans (see page 215) or 1 (15-ounce / 425g) can, rinsed and drained

³/₄ cup / 2.5 oz / 70 g sliced almonds, toasted (see page 219)

Fine-grain sea salt

1 tablespoon fresh lemon juice, plus more if needed

¹/₄ to ³/₄ cup / 60 to 180 ml hot water

Grated zest of ¹/₂ lemon

In a small saucepan, combine the olive oil, rosemary, and garlic. Over medium-low heat, slowly warm the mixture until the oil just barely starts to sizzle, 1 to 2 minutes. Remove from the heat and set aside for 10 minutes. Pour the oil through a strainer and discard the garlic and rosemary bits.

In a food processor, combine the beans, two-thirds of the almonds, a scant ¹/₂ teaspoon salt, the lemon juice, and two-thirds of the rosemary oil. Pulse a couple of times to bring the ingredients together. Add the water ¹/₄ cup / 60 ml at a time, pulsing all the while, until the mixture is the consistency of thick frosting. You might not need all the water; it really depends on how starchy your beans are and how thick you'd like the spread to be. Alternatively, you can use an immersion blender, but the consistency of the spread is better when you use a food processor. Taste and adjust with more lemon juice or salt, if needed.

Scoop the spread into a small serving dish and make a few indentations in the top. Sprinkle with the lemon zest and the remaining almonds and drizzle with the remaining rosemary oil.

MAKES ABOUT 2 CUPS / 16 OZ / 450 G

Refreshing, light, and healthy, the unstructured lemony coolness of this cucumber raita works nicely with the toasted crispness of Pita Chips (page 108). I also love it on a hot summer day thrown over short pasta, brown rice, or even farro.

Raita

YOGURT, CUCUMBER, WALNUTS, RED PEPPER FLAKES

1½ small cucumbers (about 12 oz / 340 g total), unpeeled, halved, and seeded

1 clove garlic, peeled

¼ teaspoon fine-grain sea salt

½ cup / 2 oz / 60 g walnut halves, toasted (see page 219), and coarsely chopped

Grated zest of ½ lemon

1 tablespoon fresh lemon juice

Big pinch of red pepper flakes

¼ cup / 2 oz / 60 g plain yogurt

Shred the cucumbers on the large holes of a box grater. Measure out 1½ cups / 9 oz / 255 g grated cucumber and give it a gentle squeeze to work out excess water. Put the cucumber in a small bowl.

Put the garlic on a cutting board, sprinkle it with the salt, and work the garlic into a paste by chopping and smashing with a knife. Add this to the cucumber, along with the walnuts, lemon zest and juice, and the red pepper flakes. Stir with a fork until combined, then fold in the yogurt. Set aside for a few minutes to let the flavors meld before serving.

MAKES 1½ CUPS / 13 OZ / 370 G

You want relatively short, wide pieces of cucumber here, which is why it is shredded on a large-holed box grater. If you are getting long, stringy pieces, give them a quick chop after grating.

Manouri is an unassuming cheese with an appearance that could be mistaken for cream cheese. It is bright white, rindless, sliced from a large log, and nothing particularly special to look at. That being said, one night, my friend Karen Merzenich did a simple manouri cheese plate that I completely fell for. She drizzled pieces of the mild-tasting cheese with a runny clover honey. The creamy cheese smeared into the sweet nectar on a crisp cracker was just the thing. When I serve it, I like to finish things off with chopped chives, but you might opt for a generous sprinkling of booze-soaked golden raisins or Marcona almonds.

I buy sheep's milk manouri, but you might come across a goat's milk version as well.

Honeyed Manouri
HONEY & CHIVES

Cut the manouri into four wedges and arrange on a single plate. Drizzle with the honey and sprinkle with the chives. Serve with your favorite extra-crisp crackers.

SERVES 4

1½-inch / 4cm thick slice manouri cheese
3 tablespoons honey
3 tablespoons chopped fresh chives
Crackers, to serve

This is the sort of thing I like to have on hand for healthy afternoon snacking. It has protein from the eggs, lots of greens, and fat from the nuts, so it keeps me full for a good while. I like it mounded on a thin crostini or toasted Pita Chip (page 108), wrapped in a piece of lavash, or tucked into a pita bread. And it's the sort of thing you can take to a party or potluck if you want to be sure to have something homemade and substantial to snack on.

Spinach Chop

HARD-BOILED EGGS, GARLIC, ALMONDS, HARISSA

16 ounces / 450 g spinach, tough stems removed

1 tablespoon extra-virgin olive oil

3 cloves garlic, minced

1 tablespoon harissa

4 large hard-cooked eggs, (see box below) peeled and chopped

1/2 cup / 2 oz / 60 g slivered almonds, toasted (see page 219)

Scant 1/2 teaspoon fine-grain sea salt

Grated zest of 1/2 lemon (optional)

Add 1/2 inch / 1 cm water to a pot and bring to a boil. Add the spinach and stir constantly until the spinach collapses entirely, about a minute. Drain the spinach and run cold water over it until it's cooled. Spin the spinach in a salad spinner to get rid of as much of the water as possible. Alternatively, you can press it in a clean kitchen towel. Finely chop the spinach.

Heat the olive oil in a large skillet over medium-high heat. Stir in the garlic and cook for about 1 minute; you don't want it to brown. Remove from the heat and stir in the harissa and the spinach. Add the eggs, almonds, salt, and lemon zest and stir again gently until everything is well combined. Serve warm or at room temperature.

SERVES 4

TO HARD-COOK EGGS, put the eggs in a medium saucepan and cover with cold water by 1/2 inch / 1 cm or so. Bring to a gentle boil over medium heat. The eggs should just barely start rattling against the bottom of the pan. Turn off the heat, cover, and let sit for exactly 7 minutes, or a couple of minutes longer if you're using extra-large eggs. Have a big bowl of ice water ready. When the eggs are through cooking, put them in the ice water for about 3 minutes, long enough to stop the cooking. Peel carefully.

Get your chickpeas as dry as possible before roasting. This will help prevent steaming so they crisp up.

Paprika is sold a number of different ways: smoked, sweet, and hot. I like to blend these three together with a bit of olive oil and some herbs to make this alternative to spiced nuts. Using the trio of paprikas gives more flavor than you'd get using a single paprika.

You can also keep these chickpeas on hand to toss into various grain bowls and stir-fries, or to use as the finishing touch on a bowl of soup.

Roasted Chickpeas

THREE PAPRIKAS, LEMON ZEST, ROSEMARY, THYME

Preheat the oven to 425°F / 220°C with a rack placed in the top third of the oven.

Pour the well-dried chickpeas onto a rimmed baking sheet in a single layer and roast for 10 minutes. Shake the pan and roast for another 8 to 10 minutes, until the chickpeas crisp up a bit. Keep a close eye on them to avoid burning, particularly if you suspect that your oven runs hot.

In the meantime, combine the olive oil, paprikas, salt, lemon zest, rosemary, and thyme in a large mixing bowl. Carefully transfer the chickpeas to the bowl and toss until well coated. Return them to the baking sheet and roast for another 3 to 5 minutes, until fragrant. Let cool for 1 to 2 minutes and serve warm.

MAKES ABOUT 3 CUPS / 17.5 OZ / 500 G

3 cups / 15 oz / 425 g cooked chickpeas (see page 215), or 1¹/₂ (15-ounce / 425g) cans chickpeas, rinsed, drained, and spun dry in a salad spinner

2 tablespoons extra-virgin olive oil

1¹/₂ teaspoons sweet paprika

1¹/₂ teaspoons smoked paprika (pimenton)

1¹/₂ teaspoons hot paprika

¹/₂ teaspoon fine-grain sea salt

Grated zest of 1 lemon

1 teaspoon chopped fresh rosemary

1 teaspoon chopped fresh thyme

TO COOK QUINOA: Combine 2 cups / 12 oz / 340 g of well-rinsed uncooked quinoa with 3 cups / 700 ml water and $^1/_2$ teaspoon fine-grain sea salt in a medium saucepan. Bring to a boil, cover, decrease the heat, and simmer for 25 to 30 minutes, until the quinoa is tender and you can see the little quinoa curlicues.

Anytime I have leftover cooked quinoa, I make these little patties. They're good hot or cold and are well suited to fighting afternoon hunger pangs. It's a bit of a stretch, but they could be described as a (very) distant cousin of *arancini*, Italy's beloved deep-fried risotto balls. In contrast, these are pan-fried in a touch of oil, and smushed flat in the pan to get as much surface browning and crust as possible. I'm including my basic version, but often times I'll add a handful of very finely chopped this-or-that: broccoli, asparagus, or cauliflower, depending on the season. They're great on their own, slathered with ripe avocado or drizzled with hot sauce.

Little Quinoa Patties

GOAT CHEESE, GARLIC, HERBS

Combine the quinoa, eggs, and salt in a medium bowl. Stir in the chives, onion, cheese, and garlic. Add the bread crumbs, stir, and let sit for a few minutes so the crumbs can absorb some of the moisture. At this point, you should have a mixture you can easily form into twelve 1-inch / 2.5cm thick patties. I err on the very moist side because it makes for a not-overly-dry patty, but you can add more bread crumbs, a bit at a time, to firm up the mixture, if need be. Conversely, a bit more beaten egg or water can be used to moisten the mixture.

Heat the oil in a large, heavy skillet over medium-low heat, add 6 patties, if they'll fit with some room between each, cover, and cook for 7 to 10 minutes, until the bottoms are deeply browned. Turn up the heat if there is no browning after 10 minutes and continue to cook until the patties are browned. Carefully flip the patties with a spatula and cook the second sides for 7 minutes, or until golden. Remove from the skillet and cool on a wire rack while you cook the remaining patties. Alternatively, the quinoa mixture keeps nicely in the refrigerator for a few days; you can cook patties to order, if you prefer.

MAKES 12 LITTLE PATTIES

2^1/$_2$ cups / 12 oz / 340 g cooked quinoa (see box at left), at room temperature

4 large eggs, beaten

^{1}/$_2$ teaspoon fine-grain sea salt

^{1}/$_3$ cup / .5 oz / 15 g finely chopped fresh chives

1 yellow or white onion, finely chopped

^{1}/$_3$ cup / .5 oz/ 15 g freshly grated Parmesan or Gruyère cheese

3 cloves garlic, finely chopped

1 cup / 3.5 oz / 100 g whole grain bread crumbs, plus more if needed

Water, if needed

1 tablespoon extra-virgin olive oil or clarified butter (see page 224)

Here, I like to work the flavor of Dijon-style mustard and brown butter into a big, family-style bowl of popcorn—and then really pile on the fresh herbs. The lively green notes of the chives and thyme play nicely off the assertiveness of the mustard butter.

Popcorn

MUSTARD, THYME, CHIVES, BUTTER

4 tablespoons clarified butter (see page 224) or extra-virgin olive oil

³/₄ cup / 5 oz / 140 g popcorn kernels

¹/₃ cup / 2.5 oz / 70 g unsalted butter

2 tablespoons Dijon-style mustard

Scant ¹/₂ teaspoon fine-grain sea salt

1 bunch fresh chives, minced

1 teaspoon fresh thyme

Heat the clarified butter in a deep, heavy saucepan over medium heat. Add a few popcorn kernels to the pan and cover. Once they pop, add the remaining kernels and shake the pot until they cover the bottom of the pan evenly. Place the lid on the pan, leaving just a sliver of a crack, and shake intermittently while the popcorn pops, until there is a 5-second pause between pops. Remove the popcorn from heat and transfer all the popped corn to a large bowl, leaving any unpopped kernels behind.

In the meantime, melt the unsalted butter over medium heat and let it sizzle away until it has browned a bit and is fragrant. Whisk in the mustard and salt.

Pour one-third of the mustard butter over the popped corn and toss well, about 1 minute. I find salad servers come in handy here. Add about half of the remaining mustard butter and toss for another minute. Taste, decide if you want more butter, and if you do, add to taste. Sprinkle with the chives and thyme and toss one last time.

SERVES 4 TO 6

DINNER

dinner

TAKING THIS TIME TO THINK ABOUT how dinner intersects my life invites a kaleidoscope of memories. I think of the burst of pink flowers printed on a favorite tablecloth, a wooden rolling pin moving across butter-flecked dough, my dad's hand gripping a frosted mug straight from the freezer, my mom's favorite salad brimming with juicy segments of winter mandarins. I think of nights rich with smiles and familiar voices, and lots of belly laughs. Twinkling eyes, stories shared, journeys relayed, dilemmas discussed—all of it.

I'm a believer that dinner is what you make of it, and it always has the potential to be something special. It's the time of day when the people in your life can come together to share and reflect on the day—to enjoy a meal together, however simple or complex.

Dinner around here ranges from the simplest preparations to elaborate weekend undertakings, and everything in between. Sometimes making dinner is a solo endeavor, and other times a team effort. There are countless nights I find myself in the kitchen, Wayne to the right of me; I'm chopping, he's rinsing. I'm measuring lentils. He's crushing garlic. I pop the cork on a bottle of cider. He's making sure the compost bin is under control.

On nights I cook for myself, often a simple bowl of cheese-dusted pasta is just the thing. Other nights I love nothing more than being in a kitchen buzzing with activity, kids underfoot, and conversation and good smells filling the space.

One of the things you'll probably notice in this chapter is how much I favor a single-pan or one-pot meal. No one looks forward to a sink full of post-meal dirty dishes, myself included. Consequently, there is no piece of kitchen equipment, aside from my knife, perhaps, that gets more of a workout than my skillet or my big pot.

Farro Soup | 128
curry powder, lentils, salted lemon yogurt

Harissa Ravioli | 131
broccoli, nuts, feta, oil-cured olives

Pan-Fried Mung Beans with Tempeh | 132
tempeh, cilantro, broccolini, lemon zest

Chickpea Stew | 134
saffron, yogurt, garlic

Weeknight Curry | 135
tofu, coconut milk, seasonal vegetables

Summer Linguine | 137
zucchini, garlic, parmesan, red pepper flakes

Stuffed Tomatoes | 138
whole wheat couscous, harissa, basil, shallots

Black Pepper Tempeh | 141
cauliflower rice, garlic, ginger, natural cane sugar

Dilled Green Beans with Seitan | 142
seitan, leeks, sea salt

Mushroom Sauté | 143
fresh porcini mushrooms, seitan, garlic, asparagus

Pomegranate-Glazed Eggplant with Tempeh | 146
tempeh, winter squash, ricotta salata

Green Lentil Soup | 149
curry powder, brown butter, coconut milk, chives

Cabbage Soup | 150
chickpeas, potatoes, garlic, curry powder

Cauliflower Soup | 152
aged cheddar & mustard croutons

Wild Rice Casserole | 155
cremini mushrooms, mustard, tarragon

Black Sesame Otsu | 156
soba noodles, black sesame paste, tofu, green onions

Miso-Curry Delicata Squash | 158
tofu, kale, cilantro, pepitas

I have a feisty, spicy Madras curry powder I like to use in this soup, but feel free to experiment or just use your favorite Indian curry powder. If you're worried about the spices being too strong, start by using half the amount called for, and add more to taste before serving. Alternatively, you can skip the curry powder altogether and add a few handfuls of well-chopped kale and a bunch of chives to the hot soup instead. You can use whole or semi-pearled farro, but semi-pearled farro is easier to come by. When using the latter, reduce the cooking time to about 25 minutes. Leftovers freeze well after cooling.

Farro Soup

CURRY POWDER, LENTILS, SALTED LEMON YOGURT

2 tablespoons extra-virgin olive oil, plus more for serving

2 large yellow onions, chopped

1 cup / 4.5 oz / 125 g peeled and diced sweet potato or winter squash

Fine-grain sea salt

1 tablespoon plus 2 teaspoons Indian curry powder

2/3 cup / 4.5 oz / 125 g whole or semi-pearled farro, rinsed

1 1/4 cups / 9 oz / 255 g green or black lentils, picked over and rinsed

6 to 7 cups / 1.4 to 1.7 liters vegetable broth or water

1 cup / 8 oz / 225 g plain yogurt or Greek-style yogurt, or crème fraîche (see page 226)

Grated zest and juice of 1/2 lemon (or to taste)

Heat the oil in a large soup pot over medium-high heat. Stir in the onions and sweet potato. Add a big pinch of salt and sauté until the onions soften a bit, a couple of minutes. Add the curry powder and stir until the onions and sweet potatoes are coated and the curry is fragrant, a minute or so. Add the farro, lentils, and 6 cups / 1.4 liters of the broth. Bring to boil, decrease the heat to a simmer, cover, and cook for 50 minutes, or until the farro and lentils are cooked through. (If you're using semi-pearled farro, the cooking time is about 25 minutes.) Taste and season with more salt if needed; how much you'll need depends on the saltiness of your broth. Don't under-salt; the soup will taste flat.

While the soup is cooking, in a small bowl, stir together the yogurt, lemon zest and juice, and about 1/4 teaspoon of salt. Serve each bowl of soup topped with a dollop of lemon yogurt and a drizzle of olive oil.

SERVES 8

Feisty and filling, these ravioli are tossed with a lemony harissa oil, peppered with olive bits, salt-kissed with feta, and I add broccoli for good measure. Depending on the harissa you use, things can shape up to be a bit spicy. If you're worried, add the harissa oil to taste. Also, feel free to substitute cauliflower or pan-fried Brussels sprouts for the broccoli.

Harissa Ravioli

BROCCOLI, NUTS, FETA, OIL-CURED OLIVES

Bring a large pot of water to boil. In the meantime, make the harissa oil. Sprinkle the smashed garlic clove with the salt and chop into a paste. Transfer it to a small bowl and stir in the lemon juice, harissa, and olive oil. Taste and add more salt, if needed.

When the water boils, salt it generously, add the ravioli, and boil until they float and are cooked through, usually just 1 or 2 minutes. About 30 seconds before the ravioli has finished cooking, add the broccoli to the pot, boil for the remaining time, then drain.

Put the ravioli and broccoli in a large mixing bowl. Toss with a couple spoonfuls of the harissa oil and most of the pepitas. Taste and add more salt, if needed. Turn out onto a serving platter and top with more harissa oil, the remaining pepitas, the feta, and olives.

SERVES 4

1 clove garlic, smashed

1/4 teaspoon fine-grain sea salt

2 tablespoons fresh lemon juice

2 tablespoons harissa

1/4 cup / 60 ml extra-virgin olive oil

12 ounces / 340 g fresh or frozen cheese-stuffed ravioli or tortellini

8 ounces / 225 g broccoli florets or broccolini, trimmed into bite-size pieces

1/4 cup / 1 oz / 30 g pepitas, sliced almonds, or pine nuts, toasted (see page 219)

Scant 1/4 cup / 1 oz / 30 g crumbled feta cheese

5 or 6 black oil-cured olives, pitted and torn into pieces

Slightly oblong in shape and smaller than a pencil eraser, mung beans display a beautiful range of earthy greens when cooked and are dense, nutty, and quite filling. You may have had them sprouted or as a component in one Asian preparation or another, but I like to pair them with the bright flavor of lemon, cilantro, and a touch of creamy salted Greek-style yogurt. I add a bit of tempeh to make a meal of it, but you can certainly leave it out and make this a simple bean salad. If you don't have cooked mung beans on hand, feel free to substitute white beans (canned is fine). Flageolet beans make a nice variation, as well.

Pan-Fried Mung Beans with Tempeh

TEMPEH, CILANTRO, BROCCOLINI, LEMON ZEST

2 tablespoons extra-virgin olive oil

2 tablespoons shoyu, tamari, or soy sauce

8 ounces / 225 g tempeh, cut into pencil-thick strips

2¹/₂ cups / 9 oz / 255 g broccolini or broccoli florets, trimmed into bite-size pieces

Fine-grain sea salt

1¹/₂ cups / 8 oz / 225 g cooked mung beans

Grated zest of 1 lemon

1 cup / 1 oz / 20 g loosely packed fresh cilantro, chopped

¹/₃ cup / 3 oz / 85 g Greek-style yogurt or crème fraîche (see page 226)

Whisk together the olive oil and shoyu in a wide shallow bowl and add the tempeh. Toss gently until the tempeh is well coated and let it sit for at least 5 minutes.

Place the tempeh, in a single layer, in a large skillet over medium-high heat. Reserve any leftover olive oil mixture; there should be about 1 tablespoon. Cook the tempeh until both sides are deeply golden, a few minutes on each side. Remove the tempeh from the pan.

Add the reserved olive oil–shoyu mixture to the skillet over medium-high heat. Stir in the broccolini and a couple pinches of salt. Cover and cook for just a minute to cook it through. Uncover and stir in the mung beans. Sauté, stirring constantly, until the broccolini is bright and slightly tender and the beans are hot, another couple of minutes. Remove from the heat and stir in the lemon zest and cilantro.

In a small bowl, stir together the yogurt and 2 pinches of salt.

Turn out the bean mixture onto a platter, top with the tempeh and a few dollops of the salted yogurt, and serve immediately.

SERVES 4

Mung beans don't need to soak before cooking. To cook, simply cover 1 cup / 6.5 oz / 185 g dried mung beans with a few inches of water in a saucepan and simmer until beans are very tender, 25 to 30 minutes. Drain well. You'll have enough cooked mung beans for this recipe, plus a little left over for a snack.

The alluring saffron broth that envelops the chickpeas here is what makes this stew memorable. And while the stew looks cream-based, it isn't; yogurt is used instead. I think it must be the subtle tang from the yogurt playing off the saffron, cilantro, and sweet paprika that has me coming back to this recipe over and over. If you have a mortar and pestle handy, you can grind the saffron along with a bit of salt into a powder before adding it to the yogurt. If you are using canned chickpeas, they should be rinsed and drained.

Chickpea Stew

SAFFRON, YOGURT, GARLIC

2 tablespoons extra-virgin olive oil

1 large yellow onion, finely chopped

Fine-grain sea salt

3 cups / 15 oz / 425 g cooked chickpeas (see page 215), or 1½ (15-ounce / 425g) cans chickpeas, rinsed and drained

4 cups / 1 liter vegetable broth or water

2 cloves garlic, finely chopped

Scant ¼ teaspoon saffron threads (2 modest pinches)

3 large egg yolks, lightly beaten

1 cup / 8 oz / 225 g plain yogurt

Sweet paprika

Small bunch fresh cilantro, chopped

In a medium-large pot over medium-high heat, combine the olive oil, onion, and a couple of big pinches of salt. Cook until the onions soften up a bit, a few minutes. Stir in the chickpeas, and then add the vegetable broth and garlic. Bring to a simmer and remove from the heat.

In a medium bowl, whisk the saffron and egg yolks, then whisk in the yogurt. Slowly add a big ladleful, at least 1 cup / 240 ml, of the hot broth to the yogurt mixture, stirring constantly. Very slowly whisk this mixture back into the pot of soup. Return the pot to medium heat and cook, stirring continuously for another 5 minutes or so, until the broth thickens to the consistency of heavy cream, never quite allowing the broth to simmer.

Ladle into individual bowls and serve sprinkled with a touch of paprika and plenty of chopped cilantro.

SERVES 4 TO 6

This is what I fondly refer to as a "weeknight curry." Wayne calls it "refrigerator curry" because whatever's in the refrigerator goes into the pot. I make these curries throughout the year, but I made note of this particular one because of the way the flavors and textures worked together. A bit of crunch from the cauliflower, color from the zucchini and asparagus, and spicy flare from the Thai curry paste made this one a late-spring favorite.

I happen to use asparagus, cauliflower, and squash here, but you might trade them in for peas, broccoli, and/or tiny cooked potatoes. It's an unbelievably flexible recipe, and a great way to use up any stragglers from the weekend market or CSA delivery. If you don't like tofu, leave it out, or substitute something you prefer.

Weeknight Curry

TOFU, COCONUT MILK, SEASONAL VEGETABLES

Heat the coconut oil in a large pot over medium heat. Stir in the onion and a big pinch of salt. Sauté until the onion starts to become translucent at the edges, a couple of minutes. Stir in the zucchini and cook for 1 minute more.

In the meantime, in a small bowl, mash the curry paste with a few tablespoons of the coconut milk. Add this to the pot and stir until the onions and zucchini are well coated. Stir in the remaining coconut milk. Bring it to a simmer, then add the tofu, cauliflower, and asparagus. Cover and cook just long enough for the tofu to heat through and the asparagus and cauliflower to lose its raw edge, a couple minutes. Uncover and add the broth. Stir and taste. Now here's the crucial part: You need to salt appropriately. If your broth was salty, you will need less than if you used a less-salty broth. Add a little at a time until the flavors in the curry really pop.

SERVES 4

1½ teaspoons extra-virgin coconut oil or clarified butter (see page 224)

1 yellow onion, chopped

Fine-grain sea salt

2 zucchini, cut into ½-inch / 1cm pieces

2 teaspoons red Thai curry paste

⅔ cup / 160 ml coconut milk

8 ounces / 225 g firm tofu, cut into ½-inch / 1cm cubes

2 cups / 8 oz / 225 g chopped cauliflower

12 asparagus spears, trimmed and cut into 1-inch / 2.5cm pieces

½ cup / 120 ml vegetable broth or water

This was the first recipe I set aside for inclusion in this book. And now every time the shock of garlic hits a hot skillet before being combined with shredded summer squash, delicate thin strands of pasta, and a flurry of grated cheese, I'm reminded of why. Thank you, Lori Narlock, for serving this to a tiny houseful of friends one night deep in the Mendocino woods.

I like to make this with a blend of whole wheat pasta and standard pasta. It keeps the dish light and summery. Half spinach pasta and half regular pasta is another option as well.

You can make nearly every component of this recipe ahead of time. For the pasta, cook, drain, and toss the noodles with a splash of olive oil to keep them from sticking. Let cool and store in an airtight container or plastic bag. Similarly, you can grate and drain the zucchini, and grate the Parmesan a day or two ahead of time, and store in separate containers.

Summer Linguine

ZUCCHINI, GARLIC, PARMESAN, RED PEPPER FLAKES

Put the zucchini in a colander, sprinkle with a few generous pinches of salt, and let sit over a bowl or in the sink for 10 minutes.

In the meantime, cook the pasta in separate pots or sequentially. Bring a large pot of water to a boil. Salt generously, add the linguine, and cook according to the package directions, or until al dente. Drain the pasta, reserving a little cooking water.

Just before you are ready to eat, heat the olive oil, garlic, and red pepper in a large skillet over medium heat for 1 to 2 minutes, until fragrant and the garlic just begins to brown. Squeeze the zucchini between your hands, over the sink, to eliminate any excess liquid and add to the skillet. Cook until tender, stirring frequently, about 2 minutes.

Add the pasta to the pan and add a little cooking water if the zucchini mixture seems on the dry side. Toss to distribute the zucchini throughout the pasta. Add the butter and cheese and toss again.

Season with salt and black pepper and divide among bowls. Top with more cheese if you like.

SERVES 2 TO 4

2 medium-large zucchini or yellow summer squash (about 16 ounces / 450 g total), coarsely grated

Fine-grain sea salt

4 ounces / 115 g whole wheat linguine or other thin pasta

4 ounces / 115 g durum wheat linguine or other thin pasta

2 tablespoons extra-virgin olive oil

1 large clove garlic, thinly sliced

1/2 teaspoon red pepper flakes

1 tablespoon unsalted butter

1/2 cup / 1 oz / 30 g freshly grated Parmesan cheese, plus more to serve

Freshly ground black pepper

A couple pointers here: Don't attempt to stuff underripe tomatoes; it's a challenge to carve them, and the flavor will disappoint. I look for dry-farmed Early Girl tomatoes, but any great tasting, ever-so-slightly overripe ones will do. You can stuff the tomatoes up to a day ahead of time, and bake at your convenience. I should also mention, harissa differs from brand to brand; some are quite a bit spicier than others. Have a taste of the paste first and adjust the amount of harissa in the recipe to your liking.

Stuffed Tomatoes

WHOLE WHEAT COUSCOUS, HARISSA, BASIL, SHALLOTS

6 medium-large, ripe
  red tomatoes (about
  5 ounces / 140 g each)
1/2 cup / 4 oz / 115 g plain
  yogurt
Scant 1 tablespoon harissa,
  plus more if needed
1 tablespoon extra-virgin
  olive oil, plus a drizzle,
  to serve
12 fresh basil leaves, chopped
2 shallots, minced
Fine-grain sea salt
1/2 cup / 3 oz / 85 g whole
  wheat or barley couscous

Preheat the oven to 350°F / 180°C with a rack in the middle of the oven. Generously butter or oil a medium baking dish or gratin pan. You want the tomatoes to nestle together in the dish without much room between them.

Use a serrated knife to cut the top 10 percent from each tomato. Working over a bowl, use a spoon to scoop the flesh from each tomato, letting the juice and tomato chunks fall into the bowl. Do your best to avoid piercing the walls of the tomatoes. Use your hands to break up any large chunks of carved-out tomato flesh. Arrange the tomato "shells" in the prepared baking dish.

To make the filling, combine 2/3 cup / 5 oz / 140 g of tomato chunks and juice, the yogurt, harissa, olive oil, most of the basil, shallots, and 1/4 teaspoon salt in a bowl. Taste and adjust the seasoning—maybe a bit more harissa or salt. Add the couscous and stir until combined. Use a spoon to stuff each tomato nearly full.

Bake for 50 to 60 minutes, until the couscous is cooked and the tomatoes start to wrinkle a bit and brown near the pan. Drizzle with olive oil and sprinkle with the remaining basil just before serving.

SERVES 6

The challenge here is slow-cooking the shallots and garlic as the first step. But your patience will be rewarded with butter-soft garlic that's mellow in flavor. Despite the tamed garlic, this recipe isn't for the faint of heart; it's a substantial meal-in-a-skillet exploding with spicy, peppery, gingery madness. Finely chop the cauliflower into quick-cooking pieces, not quite as small as grains of rice, but in that ballpark. And if you don't have coconut oil on hand, substitute clarified butter or extra-virgin olive oil.

Black Pepper Tempeh

CAULIFLOWER RICE, GARLIC, GINGER, NATURAL CANE SUGAR

In a large skillet over low heat, combine the coconut oil, shallots, red pepper flakes, garlic, and ginger. Cook slowly, taking care not to brown the ingredients and stirring occasionally, until the garlic cloves are soft throughout, about 15 minutes.

While the garlic is cooking, whisk together the shoyu, sugar, and water in a small bowl.

Increase the temperature under the skillet to medium-high and add the tempeh. Gently stir to get the tempeh coated. Add the shoyu mixture and stir again to coat. Cook for a minute or two, then add the cauliflower. Stir and cover. Cook for about 3 minutes. Uncover, dial the heat up even more, and cook until the cauliflower and tempeh starts to brown a bit. If you need to add a bit more water to the pan, carefully do so, 1 tablespoon at a time. Remove from heat and stir in the black pepper. Taste, add more pepper if you like, and serve immediately.

SERVES 4

3 tablespoons extra-virgin coconut oil

3 shallots, thinly sliced

1 teaspoon red pepper flakes

15 small cloves garlic, smashed

1 tablespoon peeled and grated fresh ginger

3 tablespoons shoyu, tamari, or soy sauce

1/4 cup / 1 oz / 30 g natural cane sugar

2 tablespoons water, plus more if needed

8 ounces / 225 g tempeh, sliced pencil-thick

12 ounces / 340 g cauliflower, very finely chopped

1 teaspoon freshly ground black pepper, plus more if needed

I should mention there are times when I toss a handful of both sliced cherry tomatoes and toasted hazelnuts into a pan of these green beans at just the last minute. But really, if you have the six ingredients listed below, you have all you need for a hearty, substantial one-pan meal. When green beans are out of season, broccoli florets or asparagus pieces work well in their place.

Dilled Green Beans with Seitan

SEITAN, LEEKS, SEA SALT

2 tablespoons extra-virgin
    olive oil or clarified butter
    (see page 224)
Fine-grain sea salt
8 ounces / 225 g plain seitan,
    patted dry and cut into
    thin strips
3 leeks, trimmed, sliced
    lengthwise into quarters,
    and chopped into ½-inch /
    1cm pieces
¼ cup / .25 oz / 10 g fresh
    dill, finely chopped
2 tablespoons water
8 ounces / 225 g green beans,
    trimmed and cut into
    1-inch / 2.5cm pieces

Add 1 tablespoon of the olive oil to a large, heavy skillet over medium-high heat. Stir in a pinch of salt and the seitan. Stir to get the seitan coated and brown it on one side. Turn with a spatula to brown the other sides and let the seitan get dark and somewhat crispy, 5 minutes or so. Scrape all the seitan out of the skillet onto a plate and set aside.

Using the same skillet—it's fine if there are little leftover bits of seitan—add the remaining 1 tablespoon of the olive oil over medium-high heat, another generous pinch of salt, and the leeks. Stir until the leeks are coated and glossy. Cook, stirring regularly with a metal spatula every minute or two in the beginning, and more often as they brown, until most of the leeks are deeply golden and crispy, 7 to 10 minutes.

Stir in the dill, water, and the green beans. Cook just until the beans brighten up and lose their raw edge, a couple more minutes. Stir in the seitan strips, turn everything out into a bowl or onto a platter, and serve immediately.

SERVES 4

Leeks can be notoriously gritty. To clean them, I use a rinse-and-swish method. Chop them, swish them around in a big bowl of water, lift out of the water, drain, and repeat, if needed.

This is a recipe for those times when you're lucky enough to stumble across fresh porcini mushrooms. Those earthy, swollen-stemmed beauties are my fungi of choice here, but you can certainly substitute another wild mushroom, or even common brown cremini—something I do with this dish when porcinis aren't available. But skip the dried porcini; they're an entirely different beast.

Mushroom Sauté

FRESH PORCINI MUSHROOMS, SEITAN, GARLIC, ASPARAGUS

Heat the splash of olive oil in a large skillet over medium-high heat. Add a pinch of salt and the seitan. Stir to coat the seitan and then brown it on one side until dark and somewhat crispy, about 5 minutes. Turn with a spatula and add the almonds to the pan so they have an opportunity to toast. Brown the other side of the seitan, about 5 minutes more. Remove everything from the skillet and set aside.

Wipe out the skillet and use it to cook the mushrooms. Heat the butter, the 1 tablespoon olive oil, and 1/4 teaspoon salt over high heat. Add the mushrooms and stir until well coated. Let the mushrooms get nice and golden on one side; this might take a few minutes. Then stir once or twice and continue to cook to make sure all the sides brown up nicely, a few minutes more. Stir in the asparagus, then garlic. Cook until the asparagus looses its raw edge, barely a minute. Remove from the heat, stir in the lemon zest, taste, and add a bit of salt, if needed.

Serve the seitan and almonds over the asparagus and mushrooms, the sooner the better, either family style on a platter or on individual plates.

Small splash of extra-virgin olive oil or clarified butter (see page 224)

Fine-grain sea salt

6 ounces / 170 g plain seitan, patted dry and cut into bite-size strips

1/3 cup / 1 oz / 30 g sliced or slivered almonds

1 tablespoon unsalted butter

1 tablespoon extra-virgin olive oil

12 (3-inch / 7.5cm) fresh porcini mushrooms, quartered

16 ounces / 450 g thin asparagus spears, trimmed and cut into 1-inch / 2.5cm pieces

3 cloves garlic, finely chopped

Grated zest of 1/2 lemon

SERVES 4

Sand and dirt clumps seem to love fresh mushrooms. Wipe down the mushrooms with a damp paper towel, if needed, or use a soft toothbrush set aside for this purpose. If thick asparagus is the only type available, simply cut each spear in half lengthwise before cutting it into pieces.

This dish is something I make in the early fall when the late-summer eggplants are still showing up at the market alongside the first winter squash. I make it with long, thin Asian eggplants, which I favor, not only for their subtly sweet flavor, but also because each piece retains a tender bit of skin, just enough to help each piece of eggplant retain structure.

Keep in mind, if you cut the squash too large, it will take longer to bake, and the other ingredients could end up overcooked.

Pomegranate–Glazed Eggplant with Tempeh

TEMPEH, WINTER SQUASH, RICOTTA SALATA

1 long, thin Asian eggplant (8 ounces / 225 g), cut into 1-inch / 2.5cm chunks

8 ounces / 225 g tempeh, cut into 1/2-inch / 1cm cubes

1 cup / 4.5 oz / 125 g peeled and diced winter squash or sweet potatoes (1/2-inch / 1cm pieces)

Grated zest of 1 small lemon

1 teaspoon fine-grain sea salt

3 medium cloves garlic, smashed

1/2 teaspoon red pepper flakes

1/3 cup / 80 ml pomegranate molasses

1/3 cup / 80 ml extra-virgin olive oil

1/3 cup / .5 oz / 15 g chopped fresh cilantro

1/4 cup / 1 oz / 30 g crumbled ricotta salata or feta cheese

Preheat the oven to 350°F / 180°C with a rack in the middle of the oven.

Mound the eggplant, tempeh, squash, and lemon zest on a rimmed baking sheet.

Start making the glaze by sprinkling the salt over the garlic. Chop and smash the garlic into a paste using both the flat side and blade of your knife. Combine the garlic paste in a bowl with the red pepper flakes and pomegranate molasses. Whisk in the olive oil. Drizzle three-quarters of the glaze mixture over the ingredients on the baking sheet. Toss well and arrange in a single layer.

Bake for 45 to 60 minutes, tossing everything at the 35-minute mark, until the eggplant and squash are soft and starting to caramelize.

Drizzle with the remaining pomegranate glaze, sprinkle with the cilantro and feta, and serve.

SERVES 4

Look for pomegranate molasses in the sweetener or international food section of natural food stores. Alternatively, you can use maple syrup in place of the pomegranate molasses and smoked paprika in place of the red pepper flakes.

Small Shed Flatbreads, a restaurant in Mill Valley, is nestled on a side street near the center of town and is known for their wood oven–baked flatbreads. One afternoon, I broke with tradition and opted for a bowl of their curried green lentil soup instead of one of their pizza-like specialties. I've been making my own version at home ever since. I avoid du Puy lentils for this particular soup, seeking out green lentils or green split peas instead; the latter are the color of fresh peas. After pureeing, split peas are a much nicer shade of green next to the curried brown-butter drizzle.

Leftovers thicken up in the refrigerator; just add a splash of broth, water, or coconut milk to thin out the soup as you reheat it.

Green Lentil Soup

CURRY POWDER, BROWN BUTTER, COCONUT MILK, CHIVES

Combine the 2 tablespoons butter, onion, garlic, and red pepper flakes in a large soup pot over medium heat, stirring regularly, until the onions soften, a couple minutes. Add the vegetable broth and lentils and simmer, covered, until the lentils are tender. This usually takes 20 to 30 minutes, but can take as long as 50 minutes.

In the meantime, warm the 3 tablespoons butter in a small saucepan over medium heat and let it brown. When it starts to smell nutty and fragrant, stir in the curry powder and sauté until the spices are fragrant, less than a minute.

When the lentils are finished cooking, remove from the heat, stir in the coconut milk and 1/4 teaspoon salt, and puree with an immersion blender. You can leave the soup a bit chunky if you like, or puree until it is perfectly smooth. Stir in half of the spiced butter, taste, and add more salt, if needed, typically a couple of teaspoons if you used water instead of a salted broth. Serve drizzled with the remaining spice butter and sprinkled with chives.

2 tablespoons unsalted butter, ghee, or extra-virgin coconut oil

1 large yellow onion, chopped

3 cloves garlic, chopped

1/2 teaspoon red pepper flakes

5 1/2 cups / 1.3 liters vegetable broth or water

1 1/2 cups / 10.5 oz / 300 g green lentils or green split peas, picked over and rinsed

3 tablespoons unsalted butter

1 tablespoon Indian curry powder

1/2 cup / 125 ml coconut milk

Fine-grain sea salt

1 bunch fresh chives, minced

SERVES 4 TO 6

This is a flavorful, yet humble soup that hits the spot on those nights when fat raindrops are pelting the windows, and wind is whipping the magnolia tree out back. I use plain old cabbage here, a punch of curry powder, and whatever potatoes I happen to have on hand. I call for chickpeas, but certain white beans work as well—marrow and cannellini come to mind. On occasion, I'll add a big splash of coconut milk to this soup if I have some leftover in the refrigerator.

Cabbage Soup

CHICKPEAS, POTATOES, GARLIC, CURRY POWDER

1/2 head green cabbage (16 ounces / 450 g)

1 tablespoon clarified butter (see page 224) or extra-virgin olive oil

Fine-grain sea salt

8 ounces / 225 g potatoes, unpeeled, cut into tiny cubes

2 tablespoons Indian curry power

4 cloves garlic, chopped

1/2 large yellow onion, thinly sliced

5 cups / 1.25 liters vegetable broth or water

2 cups / 10 oz / 280 g cooked chickpeas (see page 215), or 1 (15-ounce / 425g) can chickpeas, rinsed and drained

Remove any ragged leaves from the outside of the cabbage, cut out the core, and slice the leaves into ribbons no wider than a pencil and no longer than 1 inch / 2.5 cm. Set aside.

Warm the butter in a large, heavy pot over medium-high heat. Stir in a big pinch of salt and the potatoes. Cover and cook until the potatoes are tender and starting to brown, 5 to 8 minutes. You'll need to uncover and stir a couple times. Stir in the curry powder, then the garlic and onion, and cook for another 1 minute. Add the broth and the chickpeas and bring the broth to a simmer. Stir in the cabbage and cook for a couple more minutes, until the cabbage softens up. Don't worry that it seems like a lot of cabbage, it collapses quite a bit. Now adjust the seasoning, adding more salt, if needed. Getting the seasoning right is important, otherwise your soup will taste flat and uninteresting. The amount of salt you will need to add will really depend on how salty your broth is.

SERVES 4 TO 6

This creamy-textured cauliflower soup with back notes of aged Cheddar cheese, accompanied by crunchy mustard-slathered croutons, is a favorite of mine. If you're looking to make this a one-dish meal, serve over cubes of pan-fried paneer cheese or poached eggs (see page 222).

Cauliflower Soup

AGED CHEDDAR & MUSTARD CROUTONS

6-ounce / 170g chunk artisan whole wheat bread, torn into little pieces (less than 1 inch / 2.5 cm) in size (3 cups total)

2 tablespoons unsalted butter

2 tablespoons extra-virgin olive oil

1^1/$_2$ tablespoons Dijon-style mustard (see page 209)

^{1}/$_4$ teaspoon fine-grain sea salt

2 tablespoons unsalted butter, clarified butter (see page 224), or extra-virgin olive oil

2 shallots, chopped

1 yellow onion, chopped

Fine-grain sea salt

1 large potato, peeled and cut into tiny cubes

2 cloves garlic, chopped

3^1/$_2$ cups / 830 ml vegetable broth or water

12 ounces / 340 g cauliflower, cut into small florets

^{2}/$_3$ cup / 1.5 oz / 45 g freshly grated aged Cheddar cheese, plus more for topping

2 teaspoons Dijon-style mustard (see page 209)

Extra-virgin olive oil, to serve

Preheat the oven to 350°F / 180°C with a rack in the middle of the oven.

To make the croutons, put the torn bread in a large bowl. In a small saucepan, melt the butter over medium-high heat. Whisk the olive oil, mustard, and salt into the butter and pour the mixture over the bread. Toss well, then turn the bread onto a baking sheet.

Bake for 10 to 15 minutes, until the croutons are golden and crunchy. Flip them once or twice with a metal spatula along the way.

While the croutons are toasting, start the soup. Heat the butter in a large saucepan over medium-high heat. Stir in the shallots, onion, and a big pinch of salt. Sauté until the onions soften, a couple minutes. Stir in the potato, cover, and cook for about 4 minutes, just long enough for the pieces to soften up a bit. Uncover, stir in the garlic, then the broth. Bring to a boil, taste to make sure the potatoes are tender, and if they are, stir in the cauliflower. Cook, covered, for 3 to 5 minutes, just until the cauliflower is tender throughout.

Remove the pan from the heat and puree the soup with an immersion blender. Stir in half the Cheddar cheese and the mustard. Add more broth or water if you feel the need to thin the soup at all. Taste and add more salt, if needed. Serve sprinkled with the remaining cheese, some croutons, and a drizzle of olive oil.

SERVES 4 TO 6

I like to use orange cauliflower when it shows up at the market to give the soup a bit more depth of color. Although standard white cauliflower tastes delicious, too! For croutons, cut the bread into cubes if you want; I like torn croutons.

You can buy cooked wild and brown rice in the freezer or dry goods sections of many stores now. Usually, I prefer to cook the rice from scratch, but using a good-quality store-bought cooked rice can still be delicious.

 Here, I toss wild rice with a few binding ingredients and bake until the cheese on top and along the sides browns, then I let it go a minute or two more. Warm, creamy, and comforting, the casserole can be made with all wild rice, but my favorite thing to do, when convenient, is to use half wild rice, half brown rice. You get the creaminess of the brown rice playing off the individual wild rice grains. It's great. Like many casseroles, it can be prepared a day or two ahead and baked off when needed.

Wild Rice Casserole

CREMINI MUSHROOMS, MUSTARD, TARRAGON

Preheat the oven to 350°F / 180°C with a rack in the top third of the oven. Rub a medium-large baking dish with a bit of butter or olive oil. The pan I use is slightly smaller than a classic 9 by 13-inch baking dish. Alternatively, you can use individual baking dishes.

In a large bowl, whisk together the eggs, cottage cheese, sour cream, mustard, and a scant $^1/_2$ teaspoon salt.

In a large skillet over high heat, combine the olive oil with a couple pinches of salt. Stir in the mushrooms. After the initial stirring, leave the mushrooms alone until they release their water and the water evaporates, about 5 minutes. Continue to cook and stir every couple minutes until the mushrooms are browned. Add the onion and cook until the onion is translucent, another 2 or 3 minutes. Stir in the garlic, cook for another minute, and remove from the heat. Add the rice to the skillet and stir until combined.

Add the rice mixture to the cottage cheese mixture, stir until well combined, and turn into the prepared baking dish. Sprinkle with two-thirds of the grated cheese and cover with aluminum foil.

Bake for 30 minutes. Remove the foil and bake for another 20 to 30 minutes, until the casserole takes on a lot of color. If you are in a rush, you can finish it under a broiler for a couple of minutes, but watch carefully so the top of your casserole doesn't burn; it can happen quickly. The finished casserole should be hot throughout and golden along the edges. Serve sprinkled with the chopped tarragon and the remaining grated cheese.

2 large eggs

1 cup / 8 oz / 225 g cottage cheese

$^1/_2$ cup / 4 oz / 115 g sour cream

1 teaspoon Dijon-style or whole grain mustard (see page 209)

Fine-grain sea salt

1 tablespoon extra-virgin olive oil or unsalted butter

8 ounces / 225 g cremini mushrooms, chopped

1 large yellow onion, finely chopped

3 cloves garlic, finely chopped

3 cups cooked wild rice and/ or brown rice (see page 218), at room temperature

$^1/_3$ cup / .5 oz / 15 g freshly grated Gruyère cheese

1 teaspoon chopped fresh tarragon or thyme

SERVES 6

For those of you who liked the *otsu* recipe I included in *Super Natural Cooking*, here's a twist. In this version, I still use soba noodles and tofu, but everything gets slathered in a thinned-out, salty-sweet black sesame paste, then topped with lots of sliced green onions. The black sesame paste has become one of my standbys, and I typically make extra for use on salads, broccoli, spinach, green beans, edamame, even roasted potatoes. You can make the black sesame paste a couple days in advance, if needed. Leftovers make a great next-day lunch.

Black Sesame Otsu

SOBA NOODLES, BLACK SESAME PASTE, TOFU, GREEN ONIONS

1 teaspoon pine nuts

1 teaspoon sunflower seeds

$^1/_2$ cup / 2 oz / 60 g black sesame seeds

$1^1/_2$ tablespoons natural cane sugar

$1^1/_2$ tablespoons shoyu, tamari, or soy sauce

$1^1/_2$ teaspoons mirin

Scant 1 tablespoon toasted sesame oil

2 tablespoons brown rice vinegar

$^1/_8$ teaspoon cayenne pepper

Fine-grain sea salt

12 ounces / 340 g soba noodles

12 ounces / 340 g extra-firm tofu

Extra-virgin olive oil

1 bunch green onions, white and light green parts, thinly sliced

Toast the pine nuts and sunflower seeds in a large skillet over medium heat until golden, shaking the pan regularly. Add the sesame seeds to the pan and toast for a minute or so. It's hard to tell when they are toasted; look closely and use your nose. Remove from the heat as soon as you smell a hint of toasted sesame; if you let them go much beyond that, you'll start smelling burned sesame—not good. Transfer to a mortar and pestle and crush the mixture; the texture should be like black sand. Alternatively, you can use a food processor. Stir in the sugar, shoyu, mirin, sesame oil, brown rice vinegar, and cayenne pepper. Taste and adjust if needed.

Bring a large pot of water to a boil. Salt generously, add the soba, and cook according to the package instructions until tender. Drain, reserving some of the noodle cooking water, and rinse under cold running water.

While the noodles are cooking, drain the tofu, pat it dry, and cut into matchstick shapes. Season the tofu with a pinch of salt, toss with a small amount of oil, and cook in a large skillet over medium-high heat for a few minutes, tossing every couple minutes, until the pieces are browned on all sides.

Reserve a heaping tablespoon of the sesame paste, then thin the rest with $^1/_3$ cup / 80 ml of the hot noodle water. In a large mixing bowl, combine the soba, half of the green onions, and the black sesame paste. Toss until well combined. Add the tofu and toss again gently. Serve topped with a tiny dollop of the reserved sesame paste and the remaining green onions.

SERVES 4

Few winter squash have endeared themselves to me like the delicata. I appreciate its buttery, sweet flesh, brief roasting time, and streaky electric yellow skin—skin that is edible, incidentally. Said another way, there's no need to peel the delicata. So, for anyone who has struggled peeling a butternut or acorn squash, this is an alternative to try.
Here I roast yellow-rimmed crescents of delicata squash, tofu cubes, and a few potato chunks slathered with a bold miso and red curry paste. It bakes up golden, crusty, and over-the-top delicious. Before serving, the whole lot is tossed with chopped kale, crunchy pepitas, a jolt of lemon, and lots of chopped cilantro.
This is an easy weeknight meal to prepare, particularly if you've prepped some of the ingredients and whisked up the slather ahead of time. Then it's just onto the pan and into the oven.

Miso-Curry Delicata Squash

TOFU, KALE, CILANTRO, PEPITAS

12 ounces / 340 g delicata squash

1/4 cup / 60 ml extra-virgin olive oil

Scant 1/4 cup / 2.5 oz / 70 g white miso

Scant 1 tablespoon red Thai curry paste

8 ounces / 225 g extra-firm tofu, cut into small cubes

4 medium new potatoes, unpeeled, cut into chunks

2 tablespoons fresh lemon juice

1 1/2 cups / 1.5 oz / 45 g chopped kale, tough stems removed

1/3 cup / 1.5 oz / 45 g pepitas, toasted (see page 219)

2/3 cup / 1 oz / 30 g chopped fresh cilantro

Preheat the oven to 400°F / 205°C with a rack in the middle of the oven.

Cut the delicata squash in half lengthwise and use a spoon to clear out all the seeds. Cut into 1/2-inch / 1cm thick half-moons.

In a medium bowl, whisk together olive oil, miso, and curry paste. Combine the tofu, potatoes, and squash in a large bowl with 1/3 cup / 80 ml of the miso-curry paste. Use your hands to toss well, then turn the vegetables onto a rimmed baking sheet and arrange in a single layer.

Roast for 25 to 30 minutes, until everything is tender and browned. Toss once or twice along the way, after things start to brown a bit. Keep a close watch, though; the vegetables can go from browned to burned in a flash.

In the meantime, whisk the lemon juice into the remaining miso-curry paste, then stir in the kale until coated.

Toss the roasted vegetables gently with the kale, pepitas, and cilantro. Serve family style in a large bowl or on a platter.

SERVES 4

DRINKS

drinks

NINETY PERCENT OF THE TIME, I find myself drinking water, which doesn't sound very exciting, and certainly wouldn't make for an engaging drink chapter. But there you have it: I drink a lot of water.

Water is a drink I actually try to jazz up on occasion. For example, I sometimes infuse a pitcher of cold water with a handful of hibiscus leaves. I enjoy that, strained, with frozen berries over ice. When winter citrus is in season, I slice a few oranges, lemons, tangerines, and kumquats into a pitcher and fill the pitcher with ice and either sparkling or still water. Summer calls for pressing watermelon through a strainer to extract the juice and mixing with equal parts water. Also refreshing is lemon and cucumber in a pitcher of water. The addition of a slice or two of ginger doesn't hurt, either. Or, I collect interesting fruit syrups—a splash of June Taylor Silver Lime & Rosemary Syrup in well-chilled flute of sparkling water is hard to beat.

Beyond that, I'm a bit particular about drinks. I find myself most excited about light, bright, refreshing beverages. I buy a certain Prosecco by the case and have adopted it as our house wine. I love its subtle tart-apple notes and the way it dances around my mouth. I like to explore different pilsners and also saison-style beers— summery, often enthusiastically carbonated, and easy-drinking. Or, dry French ciders—complex, beguiling, and a fun alternative to sparkling wine. The heavy, super-juicy, high-octane wines with alcohol levels at 15 or 16 percent just don't go with my style of cooking, so I generally pass them by.

On the fancy beverage front, my repertoire is short and spritzy, and none involve hard alcohol. I've included a handful of those here, alongside a number of favorite no-alcohol refreshers.

Tinto de Verano | 165
 red wine, sparkling lemonade, lemon slices

Cucumber Cooler | 166
 honey, fresh lime, cucumber

Iced White Tea | 168
 loose-leaf white tea leaves, water

Ginger Tea | 169
 fresh ginger & water

Shandy | 172
 beer, sparkling lemonade, lemon wedges

Rose Geranium Prosecco | 173
 prosecco & fresh rose geranium

Mixed Citrus Juice | 175
 tangerine juice, orange juice, lemon juice

Sparkling Panakam | 176
 ginger, cardamom, lime juice, sparkling water

After a weeklong trip to Madrid, I came to think of *tinto de verano* as sangria's dressed-down cousin. It's less flashy and doesn't try too hard—in a good way. The name means "summer wine," and the drink is made from just two main ingredients: the cheapest red wine you can find and sparkling lemonade. It is spritzy, easy drinking, and much less sweet than sangria.

This drink goes down easy under a hot sun and is one of the few beverages that just keeps getting better as the ice melts into it. I like to serve *tinto de verano* in small everyday glasses; skip the wine glasses here.

Tinto de Verano

RED WINE, SPARKLING LEMONADE, LEMON SLICES

Fill each glass with as many ice cubes as will fit. Add ½ cup / 120 ml wine and ½ cup / 120 ml sparkling lemonade to one glass, then stir. Taste. It should be light and refreshing and not overly "juicy." Sometimes the cheap wine you get here in the States is very concentrated and grape-y. If that is the case, you'll need to dilute your *tinto* with a bit more sparkling lemonade. Fill the remaining glasses, stir, garnish with lemon slices, and serve.

SERVES 4 TO 6

Ice cubes
1 (750ml) bottle inexpensive
    Spanish red wine
Sparkling (naturally
    sweetened) lemonade
    or any not-too-sweet
    lemon-lime beverage
Fresh lemon slices

I serve these fragrant pale-green cucumber coolers in short vintage water glasses. Think of the coolers as refreshing, nonalcoholic slushies, punctuated with a pop of lime. I try to seek out lemon cucumbers, but English cucumbers do the job as well. You can make a pitcher and store it in the refrigerator up to an hour ahead of time; just give a good stir before serving.

Cucumber Cooler

HONEY, FRESH LIME, CUCUMBER

1 cucumber (10 ounces /
  280 g), partially peeled
¹/₂ cup / 120 ml cold water
3 cups / 710 ml ice cubes
  (about 1¹/₂ trays)
¹/₃ cup / 80 ml mild honey
Juice of ¹/₂ lime, or more to
  taste
¹/₄ teaspoon fine-grain
  sea salt

In a blender, combine the cucumber, water, ice, honey, lime juice, and salt. Pulse until completely smooth and frosty, and free of any ice chunks or honey globs. Taste and add more lime juice, if you like. Serve in a large glass pitcher or individual glasses.

MAKES 1 LARGE PITCHER

Rather than come up with a clever way to fancify iced tea by using this herb or that fruit, I thought I'd share the way I've come to enjoy it most: straight up, brewed with whole-leaf tea in a proper teapot. Loose teas are really the way to go, delivering flavorful, smooth infusions. Many of you already know this, but tea bags often use low-grade flecks of tea that are quick to release their tannins. You are more likely to get a bitter, astringent cup of tea by going that route. Also, tea likes to uncurl and float leisurely in hot water as it is brewing, something it can't do while cramped in a tea bag. I tend to gravitate toward white teas right now. Generally speaking, I love their subtle sweetness, light body, amber hue, and glossy mouthfeel. Because I like a light tea, I do relatively quick brews ranging from 1 to 2 minutes. However, brew time is very much a personal preference, and I encourage you to get to know individual teas and their nuances. Appreciate them in the way you might explore wines, beers, or ciders. Play with the amount of tea you use, and play with length of brew. Many loose-leaf teas can be used for multiple brewings. So, while I call for 6 cups / 1.5 liters of water here, you could certainly use the same leaves to infuse, say, 12 cups / 3 liters of water resulting in a larger pitcher of tea. Subsequent brews I let steep progressively longer in 30-second increments.

Iced White Tea

LOOSE-LEAF WHITE TEA LEAVES, WATER

6 cups / 1.5 liters water
4 tablespoons loose-leaf
white tea leaves
Ice cubes (optional)

Heat the water in a small saucepan to 180°F / 80°C. You don't want it to boil. If you don't have a thermometer, look at the water–it's ready when just shy of a simmer. You'll see bubbles starting to climb the sides of the saucepan and steam coming off the top.

Add the tea leaves to your teapot. If yours is small like mine (it holds only 3 cups / 710 ml), brew the tea in two batches. Pour 3 cups / 710 ml of the hot water over the tea leaves and let sit for about 1 minute. Strain into a large mason jar or glass pitcher. Pour the remaining water over the same tea leaves, brew for another 60 to 90 seconds. Add that tea to the jar as well. Let the tea cool to room temperature and place in refrigerator until you are ready to serve. You can serve the tea over ice, if you like.

MAKES 6 CUPS / 1.5 LITERS

One of the first things I do anytime I feel a tickle in my throat (or hear a rasp in my voice) is make this simple ginger tea. Each sip is both spicy and soothing, and who doesn't love the scent of ginger trailing from a hot mug? Some people like to sweeten ginger tea with honey, but I prefer it straight.

If you start with a large piece of ginger, go ahead and grate and juice all of it. You can freeze any juice you don't use in a small plastic freezer bag laid flat. The next time you want to make a cup, just snap off a dime-size piece of the ginger ice, add hot water, and you're set.

Ginger Tea

FRESH GINGER & WATER

Bring the water just to simmer in a saucepan. While the water is heating, peel the ginger with a knife, grate it, and then press the grated ginger against a fine-gauge strainer to extract as much juice as possible. If you can't find a strainer, squeeze the grated ginger in your hand to extract the juice.

When you are ready, divide the hot water between two cups. Add $1/2$ teaspoon ginger juice to each cup. When it is cool enough, taste. If you'd like a more pronounced ginger flavor, add more juice until it is to your liking. I usually add between $1/2$ and $3/4$ teaspoons of ginger juice for each cup of water—enough that I really taste the ginger, but not so much that it is overpowering.

2 cups / 475 ml water
Large knob of fresh ginger

MAKES 2 CUPS / 475 ML

A friend turned me on to this easy-drinking refresher over a spicy Burmese meal years ago, and since then I've seen countless riffs on it everywhere— from Paris (where it is called *panaché*) to poolside at the Parker hotel in Palm Springs. Bright, spritzy, and the shade of a sunbeam, you have to have a hard heart not to love a shandy. As far as beer choice goes, I typically reach for a pilsner (not too bitter or hoppy) or a hefeweizen. Opt for a not-too-sweet (naturally sweetened) sparkling lemonade, lemon-lime soda, or something along the lines of GuS Dry Meyer Lemon Soda. Some people use ginger ale, and I've even used IZZE sparkling clementine once or twice in a pinch. Mason jars make great vessels for this drink, but any tall glasses filled with ice will do.

Shandy

BEER, SPARKLING LEMONADE, LEMON WEDGES

Ice cubes
Pilsner beer
Sparkling lemonade
Lemon wedges

Add ice cubes to each glass. Fill half full with beer and top off with the lemonade. I tend to go a slight bit heavier on the beer, but not by much. It's really all about what tastes good to you. Give the shandy a squeeze of lemon juice and a good stir before tasting, and make any adjustments before serving.

SERVES 1 OR MORE

Truth be told, I have mixed feelings about rose geranium. With charming pink flowers and hyper-fragrant leaves, it's pretty but potent. Bakers love to infuse cakes and puddings and jams with it, but its distinctive scent can eclipse everything else if you're not careful. In the smallest of doses, it couldn't be lovelier; beyond that, look out.

This is one of the few ways I use it, more an idea than a recipe, really. It's just a simple way to give a glass of Prosecco or sparkling wine an offbeat twist. Be sure to use champagne flutes to serve, and make the drinks to order. It's really as much about the aroma from the sparkling wine hitting the herbs as it is about the taste.

Rose geranium can be tough to come by; but if you keep your eyes peeled at your local farmers' market and ask around a bit, you might have some luck. Be sure it is unsprayed, or, preferably, organic.

Rose Geranium Prosecco

PROSECCO & FRESH ROSE GERANIUM

Drop a small rose geranium leaf in the bottom of each flute glass. The leaf should be no larger than a penny. Fill each glass with Prosecco and enjoy immediately.

Small bouquet of rose
  geranium
1 (750ml) bottle Prosecco,
  well-chilled

SERVES 4

One other simple Prosecco-based cocktail I enjoy on occasion starts with a tiny splash of *saba* in the bottom of a champagne flute followed by well-chilled Prosecco. *Saba* is made from the must of wine grapes reduced down to a syrup. It is sweet, fragrant, and complex and plays perfectly off the tart liveliness of the Prosecco.

I'm not someone who tosses back large glasses of juice to start the day, but I do like a tiny glass of freshly squeeze this-or-that on occasion. In the winter, we get an amazing range of citrus in San Francisco—oro blancos, Buddha's hands, ruby grapefruits, kumquats, Kishu mandarins, Cara Cara oranges, and Meyer lemons to name a few. When citrus season comes around, I love to mix citrus juices for serving in small glasses. Pixie tangerines, actually a type of mandarin, are juicy and sweet, and play perfectly with the cherry-noted Cara Cara orange.

Mixed Citrus Juice

TANGERINE JUICE, ORANGE JUICE, LEMON JUICE

Combine the citrus juices in a small pitcher. Serve strained or not, well chilled, in small glasses.

SERVES 1 OR MORE

1 part fresh Pixie tangerine juice

1 part fresh Cara Cara orange juice

Squeeze of fresh lemon juice, or to taste

Experiment with whatever sweet, juiceable citrus is available in your area, starting with equal parts of each juice, and adjusting to taste. Some citrus juices are lower in acid than others, so I often balance things out with a squeeze of lemon juice, if needed. Alternatively, I like the way a touch of lime juice works with grapefruit juice.

I'm just beginning to explore the fascinating world of traditional Indian beverages. One of the most refreshing I've discovered to date is *panakam*, typically made during the Hindi festival Sri Rama Navami. If you can imagine a frosty cold, light, bright ginger beer, you'll have an idea of its taste. I make my version sparkling, and because the traditional jaggery is sometimes hard to come by (and slow to dissolve), I use whatever full-flavored, fine-grain, natural cane sugar I have on hand—muscovado works nicely. This version is also dialed back as far as sweetness goes; some versions I've come across use double or even triple the amount of sugar. Feel free to adjust the sweetness to your liking.

Sparkling Panakam

GINGER, CARDAMOM, LIME JUICE, SPARKLING WATER

1/4 cup / 1.25 oz / 35 g fine-grain natural cane sugar or muscovado sugar

2 teaspoons ground ginger

1/8 teaspoon ground cardamom

1 tablespoon fresh lime juice

1/8 teaspoon fine-grain sea salt

4 cups / 1 liter sparkling water, chilled

Ice cubes

In a medium pitcher, make a thick paste by stirring together the sugar, ginger, cardamom, lime juice, salt, and a small splash of the sparkling water. Stir until any lumps have dissolved. Add more water, a little at a time, stirring all the while. The mixture will get quite fizzy, so just take it slow. Serve as cold as possible with as many ice cubes wedged into the pitcher as possible.

MAKES 4 CUPS / 1 LITER

TREATS

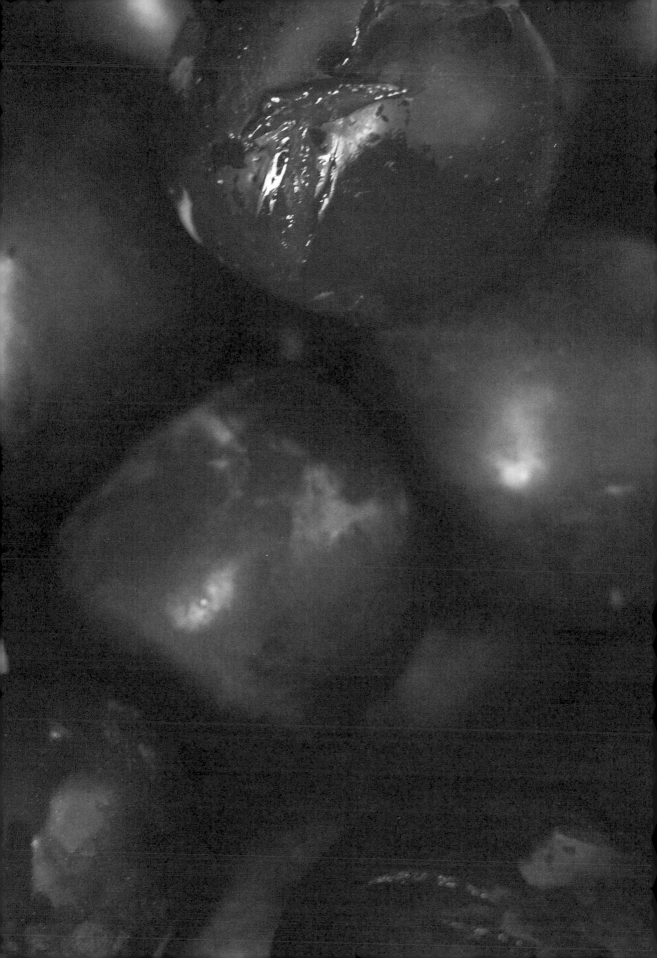

treats

I ENJOY BAKING AND HAVE SINCE I WAS YOUNG—not only so I can enjoy the occasional sweet treat myself, but also so I can share. I delight in the way a batch of cookies fills the house with the scent of buttery sweetness. And generally speaking, there are few things I find more enjoyable than tasting my way through the life cycle of something straight from the oven—particularly sweet treats baked with fruit. Everything changes from moment to moment after you pull, say, a hot peach crisp from the oven. The texture of the crumble on top changes as the crisp cools—the intensity and complexity of the fruit reveals itself in new ways at different temperatures. The way it smells changes from moment to moment as well, working its way though a spectrum of olfactory notes. It's all of these things that keep me firing up the oven and baking.

I don't use much white flour or white sugar in my baking, and I use quite a bit less fat and sweeteners in general, when you compare my recipes to traditional baking recipes. Instead, exploring a range of whole grain flours and natural sweeteners is something I continue to find inspiring. This is a subject I wrote about in detail in *Super Natural Cooking*. Using honey, maple syrup, and natural cane sugars, for example, lends sweetness to baked goods in addition to depth and character. And introducing whole grain flour, or blends of flours, can add complexity without compromising texture. The range of flavors and textures you can achieve in this realm is expansive, delicious, and seemingly unlimited.

I've included a range of sweet treats in this chapter—some are baked, others feature seasonal fruit. Some are little more than ideas to inspire, others more specific. All have worked their way into the fabric of my cooking repertoire in one way or another.

Muscovado Sunflower Kernels | 183
sunflower seeds, lemon zest, sea salt

Watermelon Salad | 184
medjool dates, lime juice, pistachios, rose water

Stuffed Medjool Dates | 186
pure almond paste

Membrillo Cake | 187
poppy seeds & sliced almonds

Sweet Panzanella | 189
whole grain bread, golden rasberries, muscovado sugar, sea salt

Carnival Cookies | 191
peanuts, popcorn, chocolate chips

Macaroon Tart | 192
white whole wheat flour, blackberries, coconut, pistachios

Buttermilk Cake | 194
whole wheat pastry flour, fresh plums, lemon zest

Ginger Cookies | 197
dried apricots & shaved chocolate

Honey & Rose Water Tapioca | 201
pistachios & lemon zest

Tutti-Frutti Crumble | 202
strawberries, cherries, currants, raspberries, poppy seeds, beaujolais

Oatcakes | 204
oats, flax seeds, walnuts

This recipe is for my sister, Heather, who has loved eating sunflower seeds since we were kids. I toast the sunflower kernels and coat them with a thin glaze of muscovado sugar. To offset the sweetness, I add a touch of sea salt and lemon zest. Snack on them as is, or sprinkle on tarts, ice cream, granola, or salads—anything needing some zesty, sweet crunch.

Muscovado Sunflower Kernels

SUNFLOWER SEEDS, LEMON ZEST, SEA SALT

Toast the sunflower seed kernels in a large dry skillet over medium heat until golden brown, 5 to 7 minutes. While they are toasting, combine the sugar, 1/4 teaspoon salt, and lemon zest in a small bowl. When the seeds are toasted, sprinkle the sugar mixture over the sunflower kernels. Stir until the sugar melts and coats them (your pan will need to be hot enough), usually about 1 minute. Transfer the kernels immediately to a plate so they don't stick to the pan. Once they've cooled a bit, taste the kernels and season with a bit more salt, if needed. Let cool completely and then transfer any seeds you won't be eating now to an airtight container.

MAKES 1 CUP / 5 OZ / 140 G

1 cup / 5 oz / 140 g sunflower
  seed kernels
1 tablespoon muscovado
  sugar
Fine-grain sea salt
1 teaspoon grated lemon zest

Frosty watermelon spheres tossed with a few slivered dates, crunchy pistachios, and a sprinkle of rose water—it's the perfect salad for those summer days when it is too hot to move. I make the effort to use a melon baller here and prefer the small-size melon baller to the large. Or, you can simply cube the melon. The presentation isn't quite as nice, but it still tastes good. The rose water is actually optional, so don't fret if you don't have any. I use just a hint of it, more for its flowery scent than for actual flavor. As with perfume, restraint is key when adding rose water. Use one small, heavy watermelon and keep it in the refrigerator overnight to chill it thoroughly before using.

Watermelon Salad

MEDJOOL DATES, LIME JUICE, PISTACHIOS, ROSE WATER

5 cups / 26 oz / 740 g
  watermelon balls,
  well chilled
6 Medjool dates, pitted and
  sliced into thin slivers
1/4 teaspoon fine-grain
  sea salt
1 tablespoon fresh lime juice
1/3 cup / 1.5 oz / 45 g shelled
  pistachios, toasted (see
  page 219) and coarsely
  chopped
Scant 1/8 teaspoon rose water

Put the watermelon and dates in a large bowl. Stir the salt into the lime juice in a small bowl, drizzle it across the melon, and toss well. Just before serving, turn the salad out into whatever serving bowl you'll be using and sprinkle with the pistachios and the rose water. Serve well chilled.

SERVES 4 TO 6

This is the easiest sweet treat I know, and one of my favorites. The key is buying good dates. I see an impressive range of dates in the markets here, but I find myself reaching for sweet, sticky Medjools more often than not. When you sink your teeth through their crinkled sugary skins and into the creamy almond paste inside, you'll understand why.
A couple of tips: If you happen to come across a store well stocked with pure almond paste, pick up a couple tubes; it lasts a while unopened. Also, if you want to dress things up a bit, work a splash of brandy or Amaretto into the almond paste before filling the dates.

Stuffed Medjool Dates

PURE ALMOND PASTE

12 medium-large Medjool dates
¼ cup / 2.5 oz / 70 g pure almond paste, at room temperature

Carefully cut a slit into the side of each date and remove the pit. If you are having trouble getting the date to open, give a gentle squeeze while holding the top and bottom ends—as you would with an old-fashioned coin purse.

Mold the almond paste into a cylinder and cut into twelve equal pieces. Use your hands to roll each piece into a little football shape. Stuff each date with a piece of the almond paste and pinch the seam on each date to seal it.

Sometimes I serve the dates whole; other times, I cut each date at an angle so people can see the almond paste hiding inside.

MAKES 6 SERVINGS

For this cake, I cut slabs of membrillo paste into small cubes. As they bake into the cake, they turn into melty little jam pockets. The batter contains a blizzard of poppy seeds and is topped with toasty sliced almonds. You can typically find membrillo paste, also known as quince paste, in the cheese section of well-stocked markets.

Membrillo Cake

POPPY SEEDS & SLICED ALMONDS

Preheat the oven to 400°F / 205°C with a rack in the top third of the oven. Butter and flour a 9 by 13-inch (23 by 33cm) rectangular baking dish (or equivalent).

Combine the flour, baking powder, sugar, salt, poppy seeds, and lemon zest in a large bowl.

In a separate smaller bowl, whisk together the eggs and the buttermilk. Whisk in the melted butter. Add to the flour mixture and stir briefly, until just combined. Gently fold in ²/₃ of the membrillo cubes until they are evenly distributed.

Transfer the batter into the prepared pan. Arrange the remaining membrillo across the top in a pleasing pattern. Sprinkle with the large-grain sugar, then the almonds.

Bake for 20 to 25 minutes, or until a toothpick inserted into the center comes out clean. Serve warm or at room temperature.

SERVES ABOUT 12

2½ cups / 11 oz / 310 g whole wheat pastry flour

1 tablespoon aluminum-free baking powder

½ cup / 2.5 oz / 70 g fine-grain natural cane sugar

½ teaspoon fine-grain sea salt

⅓ cup / 2 oz / 60 g poppy seeds

Grated zest of 2 lemons

2 large eggs

1½ cups / 355 ml buttermilk

¼ cup / 2 oz / 60 g unsalted butter, melted and cooled a bit

9 ounces / 255 g membrillo (quince paste), cut into tiny cubes

2 tablespoons large-grain raw sugar or turbinado

¼ cup / .75 oz / 20 g sliced almonds, lightly toasted (see page 219)

This is a cake you don't want to overbake. It goes from not-quite-baked to overbaked (and consequently, dry) in a heartbeat, so check on it regularly after the 20-minute mark. Served with a dollop of Amaretto-spiked whipped cream (see page 227), it makes for a rustic, not-overly-decadent way to finish a meal.

The sugar-crusted, caramelized bread cubes are what make this panzanella special. Don't limit yourself to making this treat only during raspberry season; you can make the panzanella with just about any juicy berry or stone fruit— red raspberries, blackberries, cherries, plums, or peaches. Use a substantial, hearty bread (preferably one made with whole wheat flour and nuts), and use a serrated knife to cut the bread into cubes. If you buy a loaf without nuts, toss a few toasted nuts into the panzanella before serving.

Sweet Panzanella

WHOLE GRAIN BREAD, GOLDEN RASBERRIES, MUSCOVADO SUGAR, SEA SALT

Preheat the oven to 350°F / 180°C with a rack in the middle of the oven.

In a large pot, melt the butter over medium heat. Stir in 4 tablespoons of the muscovado sugar and the salt. Stir until the sugar dissolves, then remove from the heat. Add the bread cubes and toss for a minute or so, until the bread is fully coated. Pour the cubes out onto a baking sheet and arrange the cubes in a single layer. Toast for about 15 minutes, or until the bread is golden, tossing every 5 minutes to make sure all surfaces get nice and crunchy. Let cool for a few minutes; the cubes will crisp up further.

In the meantime, combine half of the raspberries and the remaining 2 tablespoons muscovado sugar in a small bowl and mash with a fork. Keep mashing until the berries are super juicy and appetizingly chunky; this is your dressing.

Toss the bread cubes in a big bowl with the mashed berries. Just before serving, add the remaining halved raspberries and gently toss a bit more.

1/4 cup / 2 oz / 60 g unsalted butter

6 tablespoons dark muscovado sugar or dark brown sugar

1/4 teaspoon fine-grain sea salt

16-ounce / 455 g loaf day-old artisan whole wheat bread, cut into 1-inch / 2.5cm cubes

2 cups / 8 oz / 225 g golden raspberries, gently brushed clean and halved

Toasted nuts (optional)

SERVES 6 TO 8

While I prefer the crunch I get from a sugar coating, you can substitute honey or maple syrup for the muscovado sugar in this recipe, if you like. Just be sure your bread is extra stale, so that it really crisps up.

A few years back, I was visiting with one of my best friends from high school, Nikki Vecchiarelli, now Nikki Graham. She's married now with four kids, and we keep in touch mostly through swapping cooking stories, pics, and recipes over e-mail. She kept telling me about a certain cookie she made for her kids—butterless, flourless, eggless, and potentially sugarless. She swore they loved them, and one batch later I was a convert. When I eventually shared the recipe on my website, it became one of the all-time most popular.

I've since developed this carnival-themed version of the original. It incorporates whole peanuts and popped corn into the dough. You can use whatever chocolate you like—regular or grain-sweetened chocolate chips. Or, do what I do and chop up two-thirds of a 9.7-ounce bar of Scharffen Berger bittersweet chocolate (70 percent cacao).

Coconut oil works beautifully here. Just be sure to warm it a bit—enough that it is no longer solid—to make it easy to incorporate into the bananas. If you have gluten allergies, seek out gluten-free oats, and you'll be fine here. Peanut allergies? Swap them out for a different kind of nut.

Carnival Cookies

PEANUTS, POPCORN, CHOCOLATE CHIPS

Preheat the oven to 350°F / 180°C with racks in the top and bottom third of the oven. Line two baking sheets with parchment paper.

In a large bowl, combine the bananas, vanilla, and coconut oil. Set aside. In another bowl, whisk together the oats, almond meal, baking powder, cinnamon, and salt. Add the dry ingredients to the wet ingredients and stir until combined. Fold in the chocolate, then the peanuts, and lastly the popped corn. The dough is quite a bit looser than a standard cookie dough, but don't worry about it. Firmly shape small balls with your hands, about 1 heaping tablespoon each, and place them about 1 inch / 2.5 cm apart on the prepared baking sheets.

Bake for 14 to 17 minutes, swapping the baking sheets from top to bottom once along the way, until the bottoms are deeply golden. Remove from the oven and allow the cookies to cool on a wire rack.

MAKES ABOUT 24 COOKIES

$1\frac{1}{2}$ cups / 12 oz / 340 g well-mashed bananas (about 3 large)

1 teaspoon pure vanilla extract

$\frac{1}{4}$ cup /60 ml barely warmed (not solid) extra-virgin coconut oil

$1\frac{1}{2}$ cups / 4.25 oz / 120 g rolled oats

$\frac{1}{2}$ cup / 2 oz / 60 g almond meal

1 teaspoon aluminum-free baking powder

$\frac{1}{2}$ teaspoon ground cinnamon

$\frac{1}{2}$ teaspoon fine-grain sea salt

$\frac{2}{3}$ cup / 3.5 oz / 100 g shelled whole peanuts

1 cup / 6 oz / 170 g dark chocolate chips or chopped bittersweet chocolate

$1\frac{1}{2}$ cups / .75 oz / 20 g popped corn

> You can make your own almond meal by pulsing almonds in a food processor until they have the texture of sand. Don't go too far or you'll end up with almond butter.

For those who can't be bothered with fussy tart crusts, this recipe is expressly for you. The coconut crust is pressed into the pan with your fingers and topped with juicy blackberries that bleed beautifully into neighboring macaroon dollops. Don't limit this tart to blackberry season—cherries, plums, huckleberries, and blueberries all work well as substitutes. You can also substitute whole wheat pastry flour or spelt flour in the crust, if need be.

Macaroon Tart

WHITE WHOLE WHEAT FLOUR, BLACKBERRIES, COCONUT, PISTACHIOS

1½ cups / 6 oz / 170 g white whole wheat flour

¾ cup / 2 oz / 60 g unsweetened finely shredded coconut

¾ cup / 3.75 oz / 106 g sifted and lightly packed natural cane sugar

Scant ½ teaspoon fine-grain sea salt

10 tablespoons / 5 oz / 140 g unsalted butter, melted

2 cups / 5 oz / 140 g unsweetened finely shredded coconut

½ cup / 2.5 oz / 70 g sifted and lightly packed natural cane sugar

4 large egg whites

8 ounces / 225 g fresh blackberries, halved

⅓ cup / 1.5 oz / 45 g pistachios, crushed

Preheat the oven to 350°F / 180°C with a rack in the middle of the oven. Butter an 8 by 11-inch / 20cm by 28cm tart pan (or equivalent) and line the bottom and sides with parchment paper.

To make the crust, in a large bowl, combine the flour, coconut, sugar, and salt. Stir in the melted butter and mix until dough is crumbly but no longer dusty looking. Firmly press the mixture into the bottom of the prepared pan (it should form a solid, flat layer). Bake for 15 minutes, or until barely golden. Remove and set aside to cool for a few minutes.

In the meantime, prepare the coconut macaroon filling by combining the coconut, sugar, and egg whites. Mix until well combined.

Evenly distribute the blackberries across the tart base. Now drop little dollops of the macaroon filling over the tops of them (I dirty up my hands for this part), and mush and press the coconut topping around into the spaces behind the berries. Be sure to let at least some of the colorful berries pop through for visual flair.

Bake for 20 to 25 minutes, until the peaks of the macaroon filling are deeply golden. Let the tart cool, then garnish with the crushed pistachios before slicing into small squares.

MAKES 24 BITE-SIZE SERVINGS

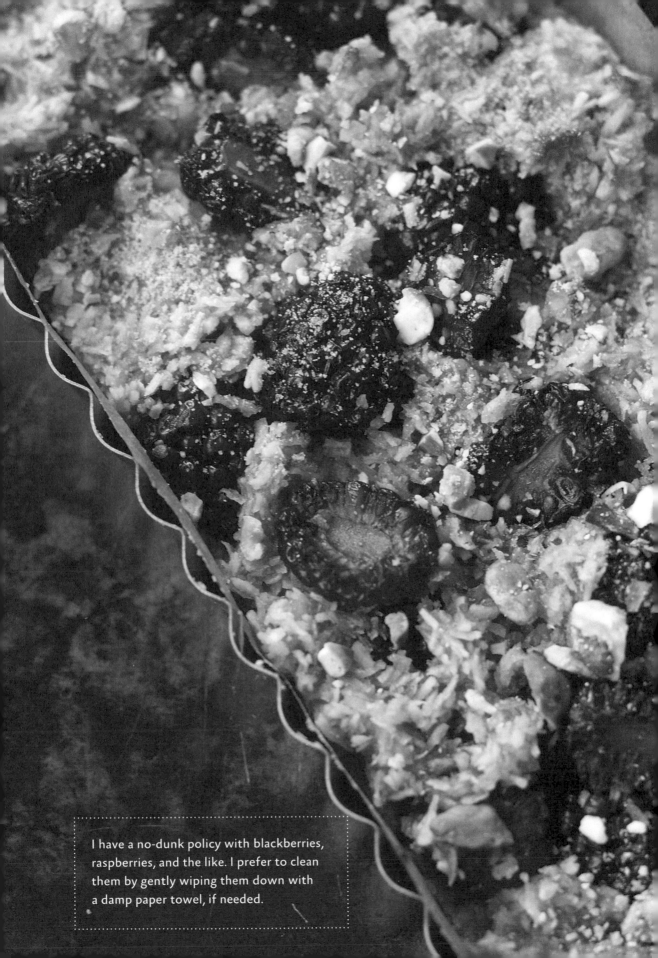

I have a no-dunk policy with blackberries, raspberries, and the like. I prefer to clean them by gently wiping them down with a damp paper towel, if needed.

If you have a preference for super-sweet cakes, skip this. It's a subtly sweet stunner that you can make with just about whatever fruit is in season. The whole wheat pastry flour delivers a pretty cake with a delicate crumb, and the buttermilk lends plenty of richness and flavor, allowing for a satisfying treat with a fraction of the butter and sugar you'll find in many cakes. Remember, cakes keep baking even after they come out of the oven; you don't want to overbake this cake in particular. It will end up on the dry side, more like a scone if you're not careful. Serve with a floppy dollop of maple-sweetened whipped cream (see page 227). Some plums can be difficult to cut. With a sharp knife, slice off two lobes as close to the pit as you can get. Cut each lobe into 4 pieces, eight total. Now slice off the two lobes remaining on the pit.

Buttermilk Cake

WHOLE WHEAT PASTRY FLOUR, FRESH PLUMS, LEMON ZEST

2^1/$_2$ cups / 11 oz / 310 g
    whole wheat pastry flour
1 tablespoon aluminum-free
    baking powder
^{1}/$_2$ cup / 2.5 oz / 70 g fine-
    grain natural cane sugar
^{1}/$_2$ teaspoon fine-grain
    sea salt
2 large eggs
1^1/$_2$ cups / 355 ml buttermilk
^{1}/$_4$ cup / 2 oz / 60 g unsalted
    butter, melted and cooled
    a little
Grated zest of 3 lemons
8 to 10 plums (ripe, but not
    overly ripe), thinly sliced
3 tablespoons large-grain raw
    sugar or turbinado sugar

Preheat the oven to 400°F / 205°C with a rack in the top third of the oven. Butter and flour an 11-inch (28cm) round tart/quiche pan, or line the bottom of the pan with parchment paper. Alternatively, you can make this cake in a 9 by 13-inch (23 by 33cm) rectangular baking dish; just keep a close eye on it near the end of the baking time.

Whisk together the flour, baking powder, fine-grain sugar, and salt in a large bowl. In a separate smaller bowl, whisk together the eggs and buttermilk. Whisk in the melted (but not hot) butter and the lemon zest. Add the buttermilk mixture to the flour mixture and stir briefly, until just combined.

Spoon the batter into the prepared pan, pushing it out toward the edges a bit. Scatter the plums across the top, then sprinkle with the large-grain sugar.

Bake for 20 to 25 minutes, or until the cake has set. A toothpick to the center should come out clean. Serve warm or at room temperature.

SERVES 10 TO 12

I do a winter version of this cake, substituting
12 pitted and quartered Medjool dates and
1 cup / 4 oz / 115 g lightly toasted walnuts for
the plums.

These are the sweetest cookies I make—sweet and spicy. I use a 70 percent cacao bittersweet chocolate to counter the sweetness a bit, and bake them teeny-tiny. A couple of the cookies in the afternoon alongside some mint tea is all you need.

It is important to use the right kind of molasses. I use Wholesome Sweeteners or Plantation brand—both are organic. If in doubt, taste your molasses; the flavor should be rich, densely flavored, and most important, it should taste good, not harsh.

Ginger Cookies

DRIED APRICOTS & SHAVED CHOCOLATE

Put the large-grain sugar in a small bowl. Chop the chocolate into 1/8-inch / 3mm pieces, more like shavings, really. In a large bowl, whisk together the flour, baking soda, ground ginger, and salt.

Heat the butter in a saucepan until it is just barely melted. Stir in the molasses, fine-grain sugar, and fresh ginger. The mixture should be warm, but not hot at this point. If it is hot to the touch let it cool a bit, then whisk in the egg. Pour this mixture over the flour mixture and add the apricots. Stir until barely combined. Stir in the chocolate. Chill for about 30 minutes, long enough to let the dough firm up a bit.

Preheat the oven to 350°F / 180°C with racks in the top and bottom third of the oven. Line two baking sheets with parchment paper.

Scoop out the dough in exact, level tablespoons. Then tear those pieces of dough in two and roll each piece into a ball. Grab a small handful of the large-grained sugar and roll each ball between your palms to heavily coat the outside with sugar. Place the cookies a few inches apart on the prepared baking sheets.

Bake the cookies, two sheets at a time, for 7 to 10 minutes, until cookies puff up, darken a bit, are fragrant, and crack. If you're not sure, peek at the bottom of one of them; the bottom should be deeply golden.

MAKES ABOUT 48 TINY COOKIES

1/2 cup / 2.5 oz / 70 g large-grain raw sugar or turbinado sugar

6 ounces / 170 g bittersweet chocolate (70 percent cacao)

2 cups / 8 oz / 230 g spelt flour or whole wheat pastry flour

1 teaspoon baking soda

1 1/2 tablespoons ground ginger

1/2 teaspoon fine-grain sea salt

1/2 cup / 4 oz / 115 g unsalted butter, cut into small cubes

1/4 cup / 60 ml unsulphured blackstrap molasses

2/3 cup / 3.5 oz / 100 g fine-grain natural cane sugar

2 tablespoons peeled and grated fresh ginger

1 large egg, well beaten

1 cup / 6 oz / 170 g plump dried apricots, finely chopped

Another favorite version of tapioca omits the rose water and adds 2 tablespoons of light muscovado sugar (or other brown sugar).

The key to this fragrant tapioca pudding is a light touch with the honey and rose water. Too much of either and the tapioca goes from being lovely, charming, and understated to vampy and garish. Choose a light, mild honey. I love the floral notes in tupelo honey, and it marries well with the rose water and lemon zest; clover honey works well, too.

Seek out small pearl tapioca for this recipe, not instant tapioca. I like Bob's Red Mill small pearl tapioca. And look for rose water in the Middle Eastern or international section of your grocery store. The amount needed is to taste, really. If I'm serving this warm, I use a scant teaspoon of rose water. But if there are going to be leftovers, or if the pudding is going to be refrigerated overnight, I scale the amount back to less than 1/2 teaspoon. Rose water tends to gain strength over time and at cooler temperatures.

Honey & Rose Water Tapioca

PISTACHIOS & LEMON ZEST

Pour 1 cup / 240 ml of the milk into a medium, heavy pot. Add the tapioca and soak for 30 to 60 minutes. Whisk in the egg yolks, salt, honey, and the remaining milk.

Over medium-low heat, slowly bring the mixture barely to a boil, stirring regularly. This should take about 15 minutes. Decrease the heat and let the mixture fall to a gentle simmer. Keep it there, stirring, until the tapioca is fully cooked, another 20 minutes or so. The time needed can be significantly longer (or shorter) depending on the size of the tapioca pearls you're using. The tapioca will tell you when it is ready, if you watch carefully; the pearls will swell up and become almost entirely translucent. The custardy part of pudding will thicken dramatically as well. Continue tasting and assessing at this stage. It is even more critical to keep stirring at this point to avoid scorching.

Remove from heat, stir in the lemon zest, then let the pudding cool a bit; it will thicken more as it cools. Stir in the rose water and wait another few minutes. The tapioca tastes best served warm topped with toasted pistachios, but is delicious cold as well.

3 cups / 710 ml milk

1/3 cup / 2.5 oz / 70 g small pearl tapioca

2 large egg yolks, lightly beaten

1/4 teaspoon fine-grain sea salt

1/3 cup / 80 ml mild honey

Grated zest of 1 small lemon

1/4 to 1 teaspoon rose water

Chopped toasted pistachios (see page 219) or sliced raspberries, to garnish

SERVES 4 TO 6

In addition to sounding fun, tutti-frutti means "all fruits" in Italian. I take a lot of liberties with the concept, and this crumble is a great example. I do a mix of cherries and berries, which are often found in neighboring baskets at farmers' markets in early summer. Experiment with whatever fruit and berries are in season where you live. The berries bubble along nicely in the hot oven with a splash of bright, juicy, fresh Beaujolais. Alternatively, you can use brandy or crème de cassis, and you can certainly use nuts in place of (or in addition to) the poppy seeds.

Tutti-Frutti Crumble

STRAWBERRIES, CHERRIES, CURRANTS, RASPBERRIES, POPPY SEEDS, BEAUJOLAIS

3/4 cup / 3 oz / 85 g spelt flour or whole wheat pastry flour

2 tablespoons poppy seeds

1/2 cup / 1.5 oz / 45 g rolled oats

1/2 cup / 2.5 oz / 70 g natural cane sugar

1/2 teaspoon fine-grain sea salt

1/3 cup / 2.5 oz / 70 g unsalted butter, melted

1 tablespoon all-natural cornstarch

1/3 cup / 1.5 oz / 45 g natural cane sugar or muscovado sugar

1 1/2 cups / 6 oz / 170 g raspberries

1 1/2 cups / 6 oz / 170 g strawberries, hulled and quartered

1 1/2 cups / 6 oz / 170 g sweet cherries, pitted

1/4 cup / 1 oz / 30 g dried currants

1/4 cup / 60 ml Beaujolais wine

Preheat the oven to 375°F / 190°C with a rack in the middle of the oven. Butter an 8-inch / 20cm square baking dish.

To make the crumble, mix together the flour, poppy seeds, oats, sugar, and salt in a bowl. Use a fork to stir in the melted butter. Divide the mixture into three portions and use your hands to form three patties. Place the patties in the bowl and freeze for at least 10 minutes, or until you're ready to bake.

Make the filling by whisking together the cornstarch and sugar in a large bowl. Add the raspberries, strawberries, cherries, and currants and toss until evenly coated. Wait 3 minutes, add the Beaujolais, and toss again.

Transfer the filling to the prepared baking dish. Remove the topping from the freezer and crumble it over the filling, making sure you have both big and small pieces.

Bake for 35 to 40 minutes, until the topping is deeply golden and the fruit juices are vigorously bubbling. Let cool a little before serving, 20 to 30 minutes.

SERVES 8 TO 10

Feel free to experiment with the amount of sugar in this filling based on how sweet your berries are.

Many coffee shops in San Francisco sell oatcakes. They tend to be shaped like hockey pucks, densely packed with oats, mouth-parchingly dry, and with the heft of paperweights. My version retains the portability of the coffee-shop variety, but with some of the less-favorable qualities worked out. These nutty, golden oatcakes are filling, slightly moist, and not too sweet. Best of all, they usually can stand up to an entire day tucked into my purse without falling apart. Be sure to seek out rolled oats, and not instant oats.

Oatcakes

OATS, FLAX SEEDS, WALNUTS

3 cups / 10.5 oz / 300 g rolled oats

2 cups / 8 oz / 225 g spelt flour or whole wheat pastry flour

1/2 teaspoon aluminum-free baking powder

2 teaspoons fine-grain sea salt

1/4 cup / 1.5 oz / 45 g flax seeds

3/4 cup / 3 oz / 85 g chopped walnuts, lightly toasted (see page 219)

1/3 cup / 2.5 oz / 70 g extra-virgin coconut oil

1/3 cup / 3 oz / 85 g unsalted butter

3/4 cup / 180 ml maple syrup

1/2 cup / 2.5 oz / 70 g natural cane sugar

2 large eggs, lightly beaten

Preheat the oven to 325°F / 160°C with a rack in the top third of the oven. Butter a standard 12-cup muffin pan.

Combine the oats, flour, baking powder, salt, flax seeds, and walnuts in a large mixing bowl.

In a medium saucepan over low heat, combine the coconut oil, butter, maple syrup, and sugar and slowly melt together. Stir just until the butter melts and sugar has dissolved, but don't let the mixture get too hot. You don't want it to cook the eggs on contact in the next step.

Pour the coconut oil mixture over the oat mixture. Stir a bit with a fork, add the eggs, and stir again until everything comes together into a wet dough. Spoon the dough into the muffin cups, nearly filling them.

Bake for 25 to 30 minutes, until the edges of each oatcake are deeply golden. Remove the pan from the oven and let cool for a couple minutes. Then, run a knife around the edges of the cakes and tip them out onto a cooling rack. Serve warm or at room temperature.

MAKES 12 OATCAKES

ACCOMPANIMENTS

accompaniments

I KEEP SIMPLE SAUCES, DRIZZLES, and toppings on hand to give flavor-packed flair to whatever dish I'm throwing together. I've included a number of these recipes here along with the supporting techniques and accompaniments I cite throughout the book.

I started making my own whole grain mustard last year, not long after I came back from France. The pockets of my suitcase were brimming with little jars of yellow gold from shops all over Paris. Before I knew it, I'd given them all away or used them all up. Instead of replacing them, I decided take a shot at making my own.

It took me a while to figure out a ratio of yellow to brown mustard seeds that I liked. In the end, I hit upon a formula that I make often. It is a straightforward mustard with cracked mustard seeds, champagne vinegar, and a kiss of honey. It's feisty, but hopefully not too feisty, and it makes a good impression slathered on sandwiches, baked into tart shells, whisked into crème fraîche (see page 226), or enjoyed on its own. Keep in mind, you do need to age it for a couple weeks before enjoying it—this seems to allow some of the spiciness to dissipate and the flavors to meld.

Whole Grain Mustard

Use a mortar and pestle to crush the mustard seeds. It takes some time and some muscle, but I try to keep going until about two-thirds of the seeds are crushed, and the remaining seeds are whole.

Use a fork to mix together the powdered mustard and water in a bowl. Mix in the vinegar, honey, and salt. Then mix in the mustard seeds. The mixture will seem thin, but don't worry about it. Cover and store the mustard in the refrigerator for a couple of days, long enough for it to thicken up. Stir and transfer to little jars if you like, then store in the refrigerator for at least 2 weeks before using. At this point, the flavors should have mellowed and come together nicely, but feel free to adjust with a bit more honey, salt, or vinegar. The mustard will keep for up to 2 months in the refrigerator.

MAKE ABOUT 2 CUPS / 15 OZ / 425 G

½ cup / 2.5 oz / 70 g yellow mustard seeds

¼ cup / 1.5 oz / 45 g brown mustard seeds

½ cup / 1.5 oz / 45 g powdered mustard

Scant 1 cup / 230 ml cold water

6 tablespoons good-quality champagne vinegar, plus more if needed

3 tablespoons honey, plus more if needed

1½ teaspoons fine-grain sea salt, plus more if needed

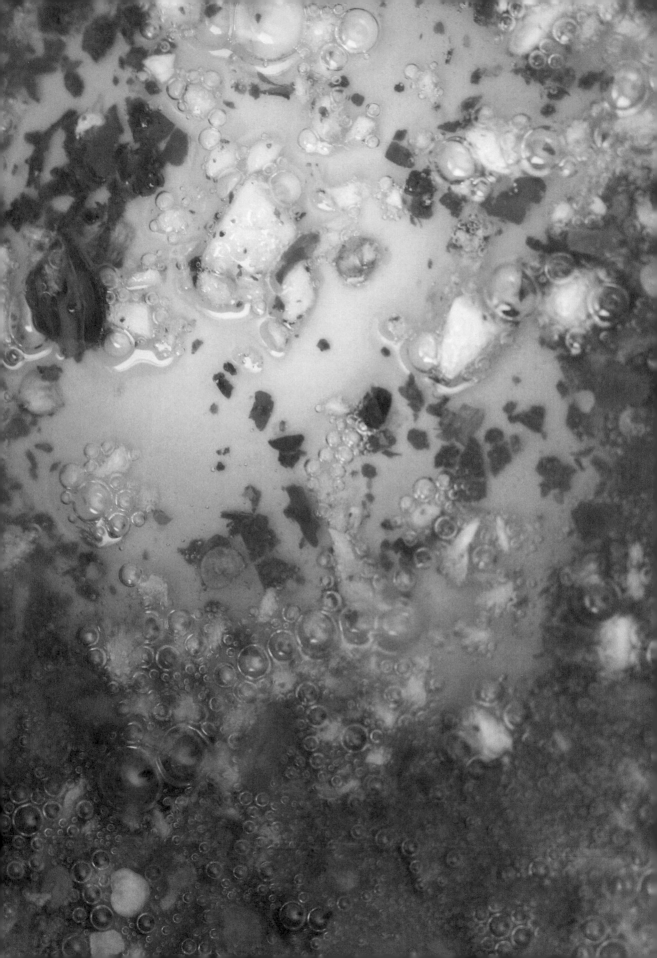

I keep homemade crushed red pepper oil on hand to use as a simple condiment and flavor accent. Sprinkle crushed red pepper flakes in hot olive oil, let it cool, and ignore it. The flavor lights up over the next day or two.

Crushed Red Pepper Oil

Heat the olive oil in a small saucepan over medium heat for a couple minutes—until it is about as hot as you would need it to sauté some onions, but not so hot that it smokes or smells acrid or burned. Turn off the heat and stir in the red pepper flakes. Set aside and let cool. Store the oil in the refrigerator if it is going to take you more than a couple days to use it up.

$\frac{1}{2}$ cup / 120 ml extra-virgin olive oil

$1\frac{1}{2}$ teaspoons red pepper flakes

MAKES $\frac{1}{2}$ CUP / 120 ML

....

I use this as a sweet-sour dipping sauce, a salad dressing, and even a drizzle over cheese plates. It goes particularly well with anything involving goat cheese, apples, pears, hazelnuts, and/or almonds. When the season turns colder, roasted salt-and-peppered potatoes pair well, too.

I've made this by hand in the past, but prefer the creamy and glossy consistency achieved with an immersion blender or in a food processor.

Dipping Sauce

Sprinkle the garlic with $\frac{1}{4}$ teaspoon salt, then chop it into a paste. Combine in a bowl with the membrillo and puree with an immersion blender or in a food processor. Slowly drizzle in the oil, and then the lemon juice, continuing to blend. Add the crème fraîche, taste, and add more lemon juice or salt, if needed. Use immediately or store in the refrigerator for up to a week.

1 small clove garlic, smashed

Fine-grain sea salt

$\frac{1}{4}$ cup / 2 oz / 60 g membrillo (quince paste)

$\frac{1}{3}$ cup / 80 ml extra-virgin olive oil

Scant 1 tablespoon fresh lemon juice, plus more if needed

1 tablespoon crème fraîche (see page 226), plain yogurt, or sour cream

MAKES ABOUT $\frac{2}{3}$ CUP / 160 ML

The ways you can use this chunky, midnight-hued berry topping are endless. It's equally at home spooned generously over cake, goat cheese–slathered crackers, and gelato as it is over oatmeal, Multigrain Pancakes (page 31), buttered toast, crepes, and tarts.

Blackberry-Maple Compote

2 cups / 8 oz / 225 g
   blackberries, coarsely
   chopped
2 tablespoons maple syrup
2 tablespoons maple sugar,
   natural cane sugar, or
   muscovado sugar
1 teaspoon fresh ginger juice,
   plus more if needed
1½ teaspoons fresh lemon
   juice, plus more if needed
Tiny pinch of fine-grain
   sea salt

Combine one-third of the berries along with the maple syrup and sugar in a small saucepan over medium heat. Gently simmer for 3 minutes. Drain the syrup through a strainer into a bowl, pressing on the berry solids to extract as much juice as possible. Discard the solids and combine the syrup with the remaining uncooked berries. Stir in the ginger juice, lemon juice, and salt. Taste and adjust with more lemon juice or ginger juice, if needed.

The compote will keep for up to 1 week in the refrigerator.

MAKES ABOUT 1½ CUPS / 12 OZ / 340 G

Make fresh ginger juice by pressing freshly grated ginger through a fine strainer.

 Most weekends I cook a pot of beans, which I then use in various preparations throughout the week. Any I don't foresee using, I freeze for later.

A Simple Pot of Beans

To prepare the beans, start by picking through the beans carefully, looking for small pebbles or clumps of dirt. Then, rinse thoroughly.

If you have time to soak the beans, do so—either overnight, or starting early in the morning of the day you want to cook them. The soaking will speed the cooking time and impart a beautiful fullness to each bean that you don't always get when you skip the soaking step. To soak, put 16 ounces / 450 g of dried beans in a large, heavy pot and add enough water to cover the beans by a few inches. Leave at room temperature overnight, or for at least 4 hours.

After soaking, drain the beans and discard the soaking water. Add fresh water in an amount roughly double or triple the volume of beans. If you like, you can add half a chopped onion (or a combination of chopped aromatic vegetables, such as onions, celery, and carrots). Bring the water in the pot to a simmer and cook the beans, uncovered, until tender. Depending on the type of bean and its freshness, the cooking time can range from 35 minutes to well over an hour. Sample regularly to gauge doneness. But be sure to taste four or five beans. I can't tell you how many times I've tasted a couple beans that seemed nicely cooked, and then the fourth bean wasn't quite done.

Season with salt in the last 10 to 15 minutes of cooking time, when the beans are nearly ready. This gives them enough time to start absorbing some of the salt. I've found that salting early can sometimes result in tough beans or beans that break down more than I like them to.

Enjoy your pot of beans on their own or incorporate them into your favorite bean-centric dish. Drain the beans you don't use within a day or so and freeze in quart-size freezer bags.

SERVES 8 TO 10

The ratio I use to cook brown rice is 1 part rice to (just shy of) 2 parts water, plus a good dose of salt. Some brown rice grains are fresher, absorb more water, or take longer to cook than other brown rice grains, but this ratio and cooking time work reliably well.

Brown Rice

2 cups / 14 oz / 400 g brown rice, rinsed and drained

3 1/2 cups / 830 ml water

1 1/2 teaspoons fine-grain sea salt

In a large saucepan over high heat, bring the rice, water, and salt to a boil. Reduce the heat, cover, and simmer gently until the water is absorbed, about 45 minutes. Fluff with a fork and serve hot. Any leftover rice can be cooled and then stored in the freezer for later use.

MAKES ABOUT 5 CUPS / 26 OZ / 740 G

....

The ratio I use to cook wild rice is 1 part wild rice to 3 parts water, plus a good dose of salt. Like brown rice, wild rice is harvested using a number of different methods. I go into more detail about this in *Super Natural Cooking*. The harvesting variables can affect how much water you'll use or time you'll need, but this recipe will get you in the ballpark.

Wild Rice

2 cups / 12 oz / 340 g wild rice, rinsed and drained

6 cups / 1.5 liters water, plus more if needed

1 1/2 teaspoons fine-grain sea salt

In a large saucepan over high heat, bring the rice, water, and salt to a boil. Reduce the heat, cover, and simmer gently until the water is absorbed and the bellies of most of the rice grains have split open, about 50 minutes. If you need to drain off any liquid in the end, do so. Alternatively, if you need to add a bit of water during the simmer process, do so 1/2 cup / 120 ml at a time. When finished cooking, fluff with a fork and serve hot. Any leftover rice can be cooled and then stored in the freezer for later use.

MAKES ABOUT 6 1/2 CUPS / 32 OZ / 910 G

There's no reason why you shouldn't play around with different types of bread here—whole wheat, spelt, oat, sprouted, or multigrain. You can make bread crumbs or croutons from any of them.

Whole Grain Bread Crumbs

Pulse the bread (in batches if necessary) in a food processor until you have textured crumbs. I sift out the fine sandy dust that collects at the bottom of the food processor, which leaves just the good stuff, but this is a step you don't have to take. Store in an airtight container in a cool, dry cupboard.

Day-old or two day–old whole grain bread, crusts removed

I generally toast flat nuts and seeds—pine nuts, sesame seeds, sliced almonds—and those that have been chopped, in a skillet. Rounder nuts, such as hazelnuts, peanuts, and walnuts, go into the oven so the heat can wrap all the way around them.

Toasted Nuts and Seeds

IN A SKILLET: Put the nuts or seeds in a single layer in a large, heavy skillet over medium heat. Toss them around every couple of minutes, until fragrant and toasty. Don't walk away; if you do, set a timer so you don't forget. I've learned the hard way after burning countless batches of pine nuts.

IN THE OVEN: Preheat the oven to 350°F / 180°C. Put the nuts on a rimmed baking sheet so they don't roll off and toast until they start to darken and get fragrant. Toasting time varies depending on the nut, but this usually takes just a few minutes. The nuts near the edges of the baking sheet tend to brown faster, so stir the nuts or give the pan a shake a time or two during roasting.

I've tried many egg-poaching techniques over the years, with varying degrees of success. That being said, I've been loyal to one technique for the better part of a year, so I'm including it here. It's a bit fussy, with more steps than you're probably used to, but I find that it delivers one beautiful poached egg after another. And for that I'm (now) loyal. I should mention that I don't like the idea of poaching eggs in silicone molds or plastic wrap in boiling water; it seems like a good way to get chemicals to leach into your food.

Allow me to back up and explain what I'm after in a poached egg. I strive for a perfect quenelle of egg, fly-aways swirled into a neat top seam. A tight, smooth egg that requires minimal post-poach trimming is my objective. I like the whites firm and opaque, the yolks vibrant, the texture of butter on a warm day. The yolks should be threatening to set, but not quite there yet.

As far as technique is concerned, I abandoned using vinegar for a while—the idea is that vinegar helps the egg whites set up more quickly, in turn, reducing fly-aways. Creating a vortex is another common approach I wasn't using for a while. This is where a cracked egg is dropped into a whirlpool of simmering water. Instead, I was quickly straining each egg in a fine-mesh strainer, allowing the runniest of the egg white—the flyaway culprits—to fall through into the compost container. Now I use a combination of the three techniques.

When I want to make more than one poached egg, I use a two-pan approach. One pan is used to create the vortex of simmering water and achieve the initial set of the egg. Once this is achieved, each egg is then transferred to a second pan of simmering water where they can finish cooking. This allows me to work through eggs rather quickly, and still achieve a nice shape to each egg.

I am including separate instructions for poaching two or more eggs.

Poaching Eggs

Poached Egg for One

Fill a deep saucepan (the deeper the better), with 6 cups / 1.5 liters water. Bring to a gentle simmer.

In the meantime, gently crack the egg into a ramekin, carefully slip it into a mesh strainer over your sink or compost, and allow some of the white to run through and strain off (if the mesh is too fine, you won't get the desired effect). This minimizes the flyaway whites you normally get. Now, carefully slide the egg back into the ramekin.

Stir the vinegar into the simmering water. Take a spoon and gently stir to create a vortex. Count to five to let the vortex slow a bit; it should be a mellow, not violent, whirlpool. Move the ramekin close to the water and slide the egg into the center of the vortex. Let it simmer there for a few minutes, past the point when the whites have become opaque. After about 3 minutes, carefully lift the egg from the water with a slotted spoon and poke at it a bit with your finger; you can best get a sense of the doneness of the yolk this way. If it's still a bit jiggly and you like a firmer yolk, like I do, with minimal chance of runny whites, return the egg to the pan for 2 to 3 more minutes. Remove the egg with slotted spoon and place on a plate.

2 tablespoons white wine vinegar
1 large egg

....

Poached Eggs for Two or More

Bring two deep saucepans, each filled with 6 cups / 1.5 liters water to a gentle simmer. Follow the instructions for Poached Egg for One, but after a couple of minutes of simmering, at the point where the egg can hold its shape and be safely removed, carefully transfer it to the second pan of simmering water to finish poaching, as above. Repeat with as many eggs as you need.

I think of butter as the quick-change artist of cooking fats. As far as flavor is concerned, there really is no substitute. Straight from the box, butter is perfect for baking. Clarified, it is wonderful for higher-temperature sautés and stir-fries. And browned, it adds a deep and rich signature nuttiness to everything from madeleines to farro salads. I tend to use less of it than you might find in traditional recipes, but I try to do so without sacrificing the spirit or flavor of the preparation at hand.

Butter

CLARIFIED, BROWN, COMPOUND

Clarified Butter

16 ounces / 450 g unsalted butter

Clarified butter is unsalted butter that has had the milk solids removed. (The milk solids are the components that will eventually burn or break down at high heat.) The end product is a pure, glorious butterfat with a smoking point of about 375°F / 190°C.

To make clarified butter, gently melt the butter in a small saucepan over medium-low heat. The butter will separate into three layers. This should only take a few minutes. Foam will appear on the surface of the butter, the milk solids will migrate to the bottom of the pan, and the clarified butter will float between the two. Skim the foamy layer off with a spoon and discard. Next, carefully pour the golden middle layer into a glass jar, leaving the milk solids at the bottom. (Discard the solids, too).

Clarified butter will keep for a month or two at room temperature and 3 months or more when refrigerated.

MAKES 1^1/$_2$ CUPS / 10.5 OZ / 300 G

Brown Butter

To make brown butter or *beurre noisette* (translated from the French as "hazelnut butter"), you start the same way you would to make clarified butter. You just let things go a little longer. You can control the nuttiness and overall intensity of the brown butter by varying how long you cook the butter before removing it from the milk solids. The solids will become aromatic and toasty and will impart a beautiful hazelnut color to the butter. I often whip up small batches of brown butter (just a tablespoon or two at a time) to drizzle as a finish on oatmeal, over pasta, or on tarts. Or, you can make more and keep it refrigerated until needed.

Compound Butter

You can introduce new flavors into your cooking by incorporating butters with various chiles (both dried and fresh), herbs, spices, or sweeteners. I typically use melted compound butters as a finishing touch on grain-based salads, savory muffins, breads, and biscuits.

To make compound butter, bring as much butter as you want to make to room temperature in a small bowl. Stir in the flavorings of choice and refrigerate. The compound butter will keep for about 1 week in the refrigerator or up to 1 month, well wrapped, in the freezer.

There are few things I love more than a dollop of thoughtfully placed crème fraîche. I love its rich mouthfeel and glossy sheen, its unapologetic decadence, the understated tang coupled with a hint of buttery nuttiness. Sweetened, it's hard not to appreciate a little dollop alongside ripe berries or a just-baked cookie. Slightly salted, it's the perfect finishing touch to many a soup or stew, or alongside a fluffy omelet. I even dip salted pretzels into it on occasion. I prefer to make my own crème fraîche, and it couldn't be easier. Start with this basic recipe, then experiment by adding various herbs, spices, mustards, and zest if you like. I use the best-quality cream I can find here, and avoid the ultra-pasteurized brands.

Crème Fraîche

1 cup / 240 ml heavy cream
or heavy whipping cream
2 teaspoons buttermilk

Combine the cream and buttermilk in a saucepan and heat until lukewarm. Use a thermometer to be sure to pull the cream from the heat before it exceeds 90°F / 32°C. Pour the mixture into a clean glass jar, cover partially (leaving a bit of a vent for any steam to escape), and let stand at room temperature overnight, or up to 24 hours, until it has thickened. The ideal room temperature here is 70°F / 20°C or so. Keeping that in mind, I try to make crème fraîche when there is a warm place in the kitchen for it to sit—when the oven is on or when there is a bright spot of sunlight on the countertop.

Stir, cover, and refrigerate at least overnight again before using it; this allows the flavor to develop and the crème fraîche to thicken further. It will keep in the refrigerator for about a week. When you're ready to make more, substitute a tablespoon of the crème fraîche for the buttermilk. Alternatively, you can start out with a tablespoon of your favorite store-bought crème fraîche. I occasionally start things off with a tablespoon of Cowgirl Creamery crème fraîche.

MAKES 1 CUP / 8 OZ / 225 G

There are a few things to know about making whipped cream. First off, buy good-quality cream. And, although it can be tough to find, reach for one that hasn't been ultra-pasteurized, if possible. The flavor of pasteurized (versus ultra-pasteurized) cream is better—brighter, with fewer "cooked" notes.

I use an electric stand mixer with the whisk attachment most often, but if you're ready for a bit of a workout and have a balloon whisk, you can certainly whip your cream by hand.

Whipped Cream

To make basic whipped cream, pour the cold cream into a cold mixing bowl. Whisk until the cream doubles in volume and holds loose, floppy peaks. The cream should be billowy and cloudlike. Go too far, and you'll end up with Styrofoam-textured cream that will eventually break.

I make little tweaks and additions depending on what the whipped cream will accompany. A drizzle of syrup (maple or other) can sweeten the cream enough to go alongside a bowl of berries or a fruit tart. A splash of something boozy—say, amaretto, brandy, or whiskey, is fun as well. Amaretto whipped cream works nicely with an almond-flecked tart; whiskey goes nicely with chocolate cake. A couple pinches of salt and a good-size dollop of crème fraîche can be whipped with the heavy cream into a billowy swirl for certain soups (Green Lentil Soup on page 149 comes to mind), so don't limit yourself to thinking about whipped cream in the sweet sense.

MAKES ABOUT 2 CUPS / 6.5 OZ / 185 G

1 cup / 240 ml heavy cream or heavy whipping cream, chilled

It might seem a bit of a shame to take a basket of the season's sweetest, most fragrant strawberries and roast them. But I have to tell you, when I've had my fill of fresh berries, this is an alternative I love. There are few things better slathered on a flaky buttered biscuit (see page 42), hot crepe (see page 50), or piece of bread (see page 96). When it comes to roasting these strawberries, you know you're on the right track when the juices from the roasting berries seep out onto the baking sheet and combine with the maple syrup to form a thick and sticky, just-sweet-enough syrup. At the same time, the flavor of the berries cooks down and concentrates. The port adds a surprise hint of booziness, and the balsamic delivers a dark bass note. The recipe can easily be doubled or tripled.

Roasted Strawberries

8 ounces / 225 g small to
   medium strawberries,
   hulled
2 tablespoons maple syrup
1 tablespoon extra-virgin
   olive oil
1/4 teaspoon fine-grain sea
   salt
1 tablespoon port wine
A few drops balsamic vinegar

Preheat the oven to 350°F / 180°C with a rack in the middle of the oven.

It is important to use a rimmed baking sheet or large baking dish for this recipe—you don't want the juices running off the sheet onto the floor of your oven. If you are using a baking sheet, line it with parchment paper.

Cut each strawberry in half. If your strawberries are on the large side, cut them into quarters or sixths. Add the berries to a mixing bowl. In a separate small bowl, whisk together the maple syrup, olive oil, and salt. Pour this over the strawberries and very gently toss to coat the berries. Arrange the strawberries in a single layer on the prepared baking sheet.

Roast for about 40 minutes, just long enough for the berry juices to thicken, but not long enough for the juices to burn. Watch the edges of the pan in particular.

While still warm, scrape the berries and juices from the pan into a small bowl. Stir in the port and balsamic vinegar. Use immediately or let cool and store in the refrigerator for up to a week.

MAKES ABOUT 1/2 CUP / 5 OZ / 140 G

I make these constantly when cherry tomatoes are in season. The tiny tomatoes collapse and caramelize, while their flavor concentrates tenfold. I keep them in glass canning jars in the refrigerator, to add little explosions of flavor to any dish that needs them.

When selecting cherry tomatoes, look for baskets of various colored tomatoes—red, orange, and yellow. I love the combination of colors, but using all red cherry tomatoes is just fine, too.

Oven-Roasted Cherry Tomatoes

Preheat the oven to 350°F / 180°C with a rack in the top third of the oven.

Slice each tomato in half and place in a large baking dish or rimmed baking sheet. In a small bowl, whisk together the olive oil, sugar, and a scant 1/2 teaspoon salt. Pour the mixture over the tomatoes and gently toss until everything is well coated. Arrange the tomatoes cut-side up and roast for 45 to 60 minutes, until the tomatoes shrink a bit and start to caramelize around the edges.

If you aren't using them immediately, let the tomatoes cool, then scrape them into a clean glass jar along with any olive oil that was left in the dish. Sometimes I top off the jar with an added splash of olive oil. The tomatoes will keep for about 1 week in the refrigerator.

MAKES ABOUT 1 CUP / 6 OZ / 170 G

1 pint basket cherry
   tomatoes, stemmed
1/4 cup / 60 ml extra-virgin
   olive oil
1 tablespoon natural cane
   sugar or maple syrup
Fine-grain sea salt

SOURCES

THIS SECTION PRESENTS a short list of sources and producers to explore when stocking your natural foods pantry. Some of these products are local to me. You might be able to find similar products in your immediate area, too. Start by browsing your local farmers' markets, natural food stores, and co-ops, and ask the people who work there for recommendations if you don't find what you're after.

ALTER ECO
www.altereco-usa.com

An array of fair-trade products, including fine-grain cane sugar that's moist and delicious, with whispers of vanilla. Alter Eco products are becoming more and more widely distributed. If you can't find their products locally, you can order them in bulk from Amazon.com; get a few friends to go in on case-size buys. Organic and Fair Trade Certified.

ANSON MILLS
www.ansonmills.com

Beautiful, organic heirloom grains milled into flours and meals.

APOLLO OLIVE OIL
www.apollooliveoil.com

Consistently one of my favorite olive oil producers.

BLUEBIRD GRAIN FARMS
www.bluebirdgrainfarms.com

Another fantastic source for organic grains and fresh-milled flours. They sell a range of wheat berries, rye berries, and emmer farro. Flours are milled to order.

BOB'S RED MILL
www.bobsredmill.com

Purveyors of a fantastic line of flours, grains, and dried beans and lentils—many organic. Widely distributed.

Florida Crystals
www.floridacrystals.com

Easy-to-find alternative to less-refined cane sugar. Widely available at natural food stores, Florida Crystals organic sugar falls somewhere in the middle of the sugar spectrum. It's less processed than white sugar, so it maintains some flavor and is free of preservatives and artificial ingredients. You can use it just as you would white sugar.

Happy Girl Kitchen Co.
www.happygirlkitchen.com

Organic preserves. They also offer seasonal preserving classes and workshops.

In Pursuit of Tea
www.inpursuitoftea.com

Loose-leaf and single-estate teas from Asia and India.

Juliet Mae Spices and Fine Herbs
www.julietmae.com

Vibrant spice blends, including a dry harissa I've never seen elsewhere.

June Taylor
www.junetaylorjams.com

Beautiful, small-batch, handcrafted marmalades, conserves, syrups, and specialty preserves made with organically grown fruit.

Massa Organics
www.massaorganics.com

Known for their whole grain brown rice. They also produce my favorite almond butter. Great wheat berries, as well.

O Olive Oil
www.ooliveoil.com

Olive oil and vinegars made from California olives, organic fruit, and local wines.

Rancho Gordo
www.ranchogordo.com

Specializing in New World foods, a fantastic line of heirloom beans, quinoa, dried posole, grains, wild rice, and herbs.

Rapunzel

www.rapunzel.com

Makes a nice, minimally refined, unbleached confectioners' sugar from evaporated cane juice. It is a buff color and tastes faintly of molasses. They also make my favorite vegetable bouillon cubes, which come in two versions: with and without sea salt. I usually use the salted version at about half strength to better control the salt levels in my recipes; typically, I use 1 cube to 4 or 5 cups / 1 to 1.2 liters of water.

Spectrum Organics

www.spectrumorganics.com

Expeller-pressed cooking oils, many organic and unrefined.

The Meadow

www.atthemeadow.com

A little shop with a big selection of amazing salts.

Wholesome Sweeteners

www.wholesomesweetners.com

Sugars and sweeteners produced without bleaching agents or bone char. Their organic blackstrap molasses is particularly good.

ACKNOWLEDGMENTS

So many of the people who helped me bring this book to light have been part of my life for years, and for that, I'm fortunate and thankful.

To Wayne, for inspiring me to reach and to imagine what isn't always obvious. And for sharing a number of your beautiful photographs of our life and our city.

To my dad, for making sure my sister and I always had a home-cooked meal to come home to—whether we were thirteen or thirty. And to mom, Heather, Mark, and Jack, I'm lucky to have all of you nearby.

Thank you to my Ten Speed family. Aaron Wehner, for being so much more than a publisher. Julie Bennett, for wrangling my words and ideas into something fit for print. And Toni Tajima, because few things make me happier than to be working together again on the design of a book; your work is beautiful. To Kristin Casemore, Michele Crim, Patricia Kelly, Andrea Chesman, and Dawn Yanagihara, for your support, input, and insight along the way.

Special thanks to the friends who have inspired a number of the recipes in this book. The creations coming from your kitchens helped drive what was coming from mine: Jess Thomson, Jennifer Jeffrey, Malinda Reich, Karen Merzenich, Olivia De Santis, Carrie Brown, Lori Narlock, Steve Sando, and Molly Watson.

A number of you welcomed the recipes in this book into your homes early on. Your honest feedback and suggestions made this a better book. Heartfelt thanks to my lifelong friend, Nikki, and the entire Graham clan—Amai, Emre, Kiah, Azia, and David—for putting a bunch of these recipes through their paces. Thanks to Lulu LaMer, Quyen Nguyen, Heather Gibbs Flett, Ross O'Dwyer, Monika Soria Caruso, Allison Yates, Anna-Lisa Palmer, Shay Curley, and Britta Garcia.

Thanks to Owen Seitel, Amie Ahlers, Gwen McGill, Lanha Hong-Poretta, Yotam Ottolenghi, Dorie Greenspan, Melissa Clark, and Kim Boyce. And thank you to all of the 101 Cookbooks readers—the way you build on ideas and make recipes work in your own lives and kitchens is continually inspiring to me.

INDEX